Triumphant Journey

The Saga of Bobby Jones

(1902-1971)

HOLT, RINEHART and WINSTON   NEW YORK

TRIUMPHANT JOURNEY

and the Grand Slam of Golf

by DICK MILLER

Published by Holt, Rinehart and Winston,
383 Madison Avenue, New York, New York 10017.

Published simultaneously in Canada by Holt, Rinehart and
Winston of Canada, Limited.

Reprinted in 1991 by

the
booĸlegger

13100 Grass Valley Ave.
Grass Valley, California 95945

LIBRARY OF CONGRESS CATALOGING IN PUBLICATION DATA

Miller, Dick, 1936–
  Triumphant journey.

  Includes index.
  1. Jones, Robert Tyre, 1902–1971.   2. Golfers—
United States—Biography.   I. Title.
GV964.J6M54   796.352′092′4 [B]   80-10834

ISBN: 0-03-045331-3

First Edition
Designer: A. Christopher Simon
Printed in the United States of America

10 9 8 7 6 5 4 3 2 1

Grateful acknowledgments are made to the following publishing companies for per-
mission to reprint various sentences and paragraphs: Random House, *The World of
Golf,* Copyright © 1962 by Charles Price; Alfred A. Knopf, *Farewell to Sport,* Copy-
right 1938, renewed 1966 by Paul Gallico; Doubleday & Company, Inc., *Golf Is My
Game,* Copyright © 1960 by Robert Tyre Jones; Doubleday & Company, Inc., *Bobby
Jones on Golf,* Copyright © 1966 by Robert Tyre Jones.

PHOTO CREDITS (by photo number)

United States Golf Association: 1, 2, 3, 4, 5, 7, 9, 11, 12, 14, 16, 21, 30, 31, 44. *Wide
World Photos:* 6, 10, 37, 38, 40, 42. *United Press International:* 8, 13, 15, 19, 24, 25,
28, 32, 34, 36, 41, 43, 45. *The Bettmann Archive, Inc.:* 17, 18, 20, 22, 23, 26, 27, 29,
33, 35. *Frank Christian:* 39.

FRONT COVER PORTRAIT - Royal Lytham and St. Annes Golf Club

For Frank Zachary

Contents

Acknowledgments

No book is solely a labor of love no matter how dear the subject is to the author. The task of planning and researching this book was made more pleasurable by the hundreds of people I interviewed who generously cooperated, understood my point of view, and furnished support.

I am deeply appreciative of the boundless patience and thoughtfulness expressed by the Jones family during the hundreds of hours spent with me. Particularly, I am indebted to Clara Black, Bobby Jones's only surviving child, who tirelessly answered so many questions, and who from the beginning believed in this project, offered wonderful assistance, and was a constant source of encouragement.

Other members of the Jones family who provided thoughtful, intelligent insights were Frances Massey Jones and two of her children, Bob Jones IV and particularly Mary Jones. A special thanks also to Carl Hood and Lewis Jones, who provided me with so much of the early history of the Jones family.

Those who were invaluable concerning Jones's business and civic interests were Eugene Branch and Francis M. Bird of the Atlanta law firm of Jones, Bird and Howell; and Joe Jones of The Coca-Cola Company, who graciously paved the way for me to interview many people connected with Coca-Cola, Walter Susong and Morton S. Hodgson among them.

In dealing with Jones's illness, I am most indebted to Dr. Ralph Murphy, Jones's physician, and Dr. Lewis P. Rowland, chairman of the Department of Neurology of the College of Physicians and Surgeons of Columbia University, both of whom read part of the manuscript and helped to clarify so many pertinent medical points. I am also grateful to Dr. Robert Burke, chief resident of neurology of the College of Physicians and Surgeons, who helped me to understand the nature of syringomyelia.

For anyone writing about golf in the United States, it would be almost too laborsome to do without the help and facilities of the United States Golf Association. So to its executive director, P. J. Boatwright, Jr., I'd like to express much gratitude and extend very special thanks to its assistant director, Frank Hannigan, one of the most knowledgeable people in golf, and to the USGA's librarian and museum curator, Janet Seagle, a special friend, whose unending assistance makes writing about golf more joyous and rewarding.

The following people contributed vastly to my understanding of Jones's personality, his golfing days, and the other people of the Golden Age of Sport: Eugene Black, Alec Campbell, William Campbell, Mr. and Mrs. Joseph C. Dey, Dick Garlington, Ross Goodner, Isaac Grainger, Watts Gunn, Richard Heilman, Bill Inglish, Mrs. Eugene Homans, Meredith Jack, George Keeler, Al Laney, Charlie Price, Howard Rexford, Harold Sergent, Charlie Seaver, Ross Somerville, Jess Sweetser, William Varner, and Charlie Yates.

A very special thanks and the deepest appreciation to the following people: Herbert Warren Wind, America's foremost golfing authority, whose wise counseling on this project and so many others I sincerely treasure; my editor, Donald Hutter, for his patience, sensitivity, and brilliant editorial skill; and last but not least, my typist Roma Sfreddo, a fine person and a great typist.

Acknowledgments

Among those who aided me in my newspaper and periodical research, I am sincerely grateful to Denise Grant, promotion assistant of the *Atlanta Journal and Constitution*, and to Theo Tarter, librarian of Conde Nast, Inc., who graciously let me use their library for weeks as I read through issues of the *American Golfer* and *Vanity Fair*.

Of the hundreds of magazines, pamphlets, newspapers, and books I consulted in my research, one magazine and five books deserve special mention. The magazine is the *American Golfer*, first edited by Walter Travis and later by Grantland Rice. The five books are: *Down the Fairway*, by Bobby Jones and O. B. Keeler (Minton, Balch, 1927); *Golf Is My Game*, by Bobby Jones (Doubleday & Company, Inc., 1960); *Bobby Jones on Golf*, by Bobby Jones (Doubleday & Company, Inc., 1966); *The World of Golf*, by Charles Price (Random House, 1962); and *The Story of American Golf*, by Herbert Warren Wind (Alfred A. Knopf, Inc., 1976). They are all part of the great timber of golfing literature.

Author's Note

To keep with the authenticity of the time in which Bobby Jones played golf, several words that now are antiquated or an infrequent part of present-day golfing vocabulary have been used. I hope the following brief definitions will help clarify the narrative.

Up until the mid-1930s, golf clubs were named rather than numbered. A driver then was called a driver, but a 2-wood was called a brassie, a 3-wood a spoon. The irons were named accordingly: 2-iron, mid-iron; 3-iron, mid-mashie; 4-iron, mashie iron; 5-iron, mashie; 6-iron, spade mashie; 7-iron, mashie niblick; 8-iron, pitching niblick; 9-iron, niblick.

Since Bobby Jones won six of his thirteen major championships at match play, several of which are covered thoroughly in the text, it deserves a brief introduction at this point. Match play is a competition by holes. The winner of the first hole is said to be 1 up, no matter by how many strokes he has beaten his opponent. When both players have played a hole in the same number of strokes, a hole is halved. When one player has won as many holes as there are left to play, he is dormied.

Author's Note

When Jones competed a very important part of match play was the stymie. When an opponent's ball was in the line of the other player's putt, it was said that the player farthest from the hole had been laid a stymie.

Of all the words that have been part of the golfing vocabulary, only the word stymie has been properly incorporated into everyday English. Its meaning carries the original terse definition. When one says one is stymied, one is directly blocked from one's goal by an unwanted object.

New York City, 1980   DICK MILLER

PART ONE

The Triumph

1

He was an only child. He was born an invalid and died an invalid. For his first five years, he was frail and sickly with an oversized head and small spindly legs. He suffered so severely from a digestive ailment that six doctors diagnosed his condition as all but hopeless, doubting he would live through his fifth year. His diet consisted almost entirely of egg whites and pabulum. He spent those years housebound, watched over carefully by his parents and a nursemaid, denied the joy of a single playmate.

For his last twenty-two years, he was a cripple who went from using one hickory cane, to two with leg braces, and finally to being permanently implanted in a wheelchair. His body had withered to under 100 pounds, with his skin draped loosely and tonelessly over an inert body of distorted bones that appeared too frail to support his leonine head. His admirers all over the world were in the millions, his friends in the thousands.

For those who saw him regularly at that time, he remained a constant source of inspiration, more than he had been in his youth when, as a part-time athlete, he had conquered all the worlds he had set out to conquer. What was still there, stronger than ever, was the man's character, honed by competition, with an indomitable will to live, and to live in dignity. He knew as did his friends that his body was deteriorating more and more each day by syringomyelia, a rare spinal disease, rarer even than amyotrophic lateral sclerosis, often referred to as Lou Gehrig's disease. Yet he faced the inevitable with a spirit that rose above his illness, so few people knew how very ill he was. His laughter refused to die—it was still young and spontaneous, always seeming to burst forth at just the right time to ease a guest at an awkward moment and chase away any feeling of pity one might have for him.

His body then was stuffed with codeine to deaden the daily pain. His feet and ankles had turned purple from lack of circulation and were swollen to four times their normal size. His hands were too twisted and gnarled even to strike a match to light a cigarette, and too weak and atrophied to pick up a glass of water.

It seemed almost impossible to comprehend that this had once been a body of exceptional strength, with coordination as pure and graceful as a leaping cat. It was the same body that had withstood more strain than ten men experience in a lifetime, for he had been a man who had battled so hard, who had been willing to accept so many burdens and responsibilities, that before he was thirty his nerves had been stretched to their limits.

4

For fifteen years, from 1916 to 1930, he competed as an athlete. For the last eight of those years, he was the very best performer in the world at what he did. In the Golden Age of Sport, his name shone the brightest.

Most of the world called him Bobby. His mother called him Robert, his father called him Rob, and he insisted that his friends call him Bob. To the British he was Bonnie Bobby. His full name was Robert Tyre Jones, Jr.

He was born in Atlanta, Georgia, on St. Patrick's Day, March 17, 1902. Except for two years spent studying at Harvard University and six months in Hollywood starring in movies, he lived his life entirely in Atlanta, a city he loved. He died there, painlessly and at last at peace, on December 18, 1971, no more than eight miles from where he was born. He was buried two days later in Atlanta's Oakland Cemetery, where so many of that city's brightest sons and daughters have been laid to rest: Margaret Mitchell, author of *Gone With the Wind*; Joe E. Brown, Georgia's governor during the Civil War; General of the Confederacy Wright Iverson; former Governor Hoke Smith. At the head of the grave was an arrangement of roses and white blossoms from the members of Augusta National Golf Club, which was founded by Bobby Jones in 1931. Alongside the grave was a golden flowered T signifying Jones's allegiance to his alma mater Georgia Tech. The brief afternoon graveside service was as he wished—private, only for his family. It was symbolic of the way he lived. A noisy ending would have been unkind and unthinkable.

The cemetery was bathed in a warm December sun, the sky was a clear, sparkling blue. It was just the kind of day when, perhaps, six decades earlier, an apple-cheeked kid in knickers might have said to a friend, "Hot damn, we don't have many days like this in December. Let's get our clubs and go on over to East Lake course. We can get in at least nine or a quick eighteen holes."

At the age of fourteen, Bobby Jones played in his first major golf championship. In September 1916, wearing long trousers at last and a candy-striped red-and-white bow tie, he competed in the U.S. Amateur at the Merion Cricket Club in Ardmore, Pennsylvania, just outside Philadelphia. He fought his way to the quarter-finals, the youngest player in the championship's history to go so far. And it was at Merion fourteen years later, at the age of twenty-eight, that Bobby Jones played in his last major championship, in the 1930 U.S. Amateur.

No golfer ever has played out of a greater fear of losing than did Jones preparing and playing for that title. He was the beloved hero from whom wonders were always expected—and so often achieved. That September at Merion Jones not only was trying to win an unprecedented fifth U.S. Amateur title, but more importantly, he was trying to pull off that final trick that would reign forever as the greatest sporting feat of his age. It would become, in fact, sport's invincible feat.

A five-month journey was ending. From May 1930 until those last two weeks in September, Jones had been embarked on an unprecedented quest. It seemed impossible: to capture the Open and Amateur championships of Great Britain and the United States—four major golf championships in one year.

No golfer, either professional or amateur, had won more than two major championships in one year, and only Jones himself had won both the British and the United States Opens in a single year. Way back in 1911, England's great Harold Hilton had captured both the British and United States Amateur titles, and in 1916 the remarkable Chick

Evans had won the Amateur and Open championships of the United States. Such precedent would have inhibited any other golfer and brought out a half dozen kinks in his swing, but Bobby Jones wasn't any other golfer.

He had never been formally taught how to play golf. Initially he learned by mimicking, then simply by playing and playing and figuring things out for himself. In his whole life he had no more than a total of ten hours of actual lessons. He rarely practiced, and when he did it was usually just his putting. Even then he only worked on putts from twelve to fifteen feet from the cup, as that was where he expected his approach shots to be. Few golfers have trusted their swing more than Bobby Jones trusted his.

Often he would go three or four months without playing, then go out and shoot par or better. Sometimes when he was forced to play for more than a week straight, the sensitive skin on his hands would blister and be scraped raw. He played wearing bandages. Every contest he played in, whether it was for a one-dollar nassau or a national title, Jones went all out. He believed golf was a game meant to be played as a contest worthy of the best a person could give.

In essence, Bobby Jones was a genius at golf. The game was in his bones. When he was eleven years old, he shot an 80 on a course measuring over 6,500 yards. At the age of fourteen, he could drive a golf ball consistently 250 yards. Yet for all his genius, Jones suffered and agonized over many of the same problems as the average golfer. While his great shots (and there were so many) stayed with him in a wonderful golden haze, it was his bad shots he couldn't forget; they haunted him. Jones always felt dogged by the terrible specter of the three-putt green, this by one of the greatest putters the game has known.

Most of the time, however, golf was for Jones the most beguiling of games. When he was playing well he easily could be drawn into a state of euphoric complacency. Sometimes, just when it appeared he was in complete command of a tournament, and the only thing he had to do was continue swinging and keeping his head still, suddenly disaster would strike. An easy par would become a double bogey. Ironically, Jones often was at his worst when the going was good.

He was always fighting against "becoming frantic on one hand and overconfident on the other." No one would have guessed there was such inner turmoil, for Jones was the player of consummate grace. While his face exuded placidity, it was a deceptive appearance that other golfers, and the gallery, misread as easily as they might misread a 10-foot downhill putt. An intense, high-strung man by nature, Jones could hold his putter for a final, crucial putt with the steadiness and sureness of a surgeon holding a scalpel, about to make a deft, bloodsearing incision. Then, after holing the final putt, Jones's fingers would tremble too much for him even to untie his necktie. This competitive spirit, of being at once both sides of a flipped coin in flight, had earned Jones the paradoxical description of "playing golf with courageous timidity."

As the 1930 U.S. Amateur approached, Jones began carrying a special burden—that of a whole nation's worship, a popular love even greater than that for Charles Lindbergh. In 1930 Americans viewed Merion as more than a golf course, and the U.S. Amateur as more than a golf tournament. It was a battleground of hope for a people experiencing the dread of the Depression. Jones held the promise of man fulfilling his greatest potential against staggering odds.

Already, Jones and his deeds had become burned into the national consciousness. The very euphony of the name Bobby

Jones had a wonderful all-American sound to it that even non-golfers warmed to. Without a shred of pretense, he fitted perfectly the mold Americans in the 1920s cast of their heroes: a person of natural courtesy and modesty who had overcome a personal struggle to achieve a singular triumph.

Then there was his physical presence. In 1930 Jones stood just over five feet eight inches tall and weighed a stocky 170 pounds. He had a barrel chest, a broad muscular back, and short thick legs as sturdy as tree trunks. His large head would have seemed more fitting on a man a foot taller. His light brown hair was slicked down and, in the fashion of the time, parted in the middle above a high, broad forehead. His eyes were a pale, blue gray, as indecipherable as the sea. His strong bony nose was straight, and there always seemed to be an impish expression about his full mouth. It was a face women found sensual, movie producers intriguing, and opponents disconcerting.

At the start of a match, Jones would approach his opponent, look him straight in the eyes, shake his hand, and offer a quizzical smile which implied good luck. If the opponent looked at the smile long enough, however, its meaning became clearer. It said: good luck, you're going to need it because I'm going to try to beat the hell out of you today. Characteristically, it would take several holes for an opponent to comprehend that Jones was being more than charming, and by then it was usually too late. Jones would be playing along at par or under, for it was really par that was his opponent, his true enemy. As the great British golf writer, Bernard Darwin, the grandson of the evolutionist, Charles Darwin, once wrote about Jones, "It seems paradoxical, but it is probably true that the way to obtain a great reputation as a fighter is to forget that you have an enemy—or at any rate an earthly one."

9

From 1923, when Jones won his first U.S. Open, it had been Jones versus the field. The record was colossal. In major championships, Jones had won the U.S. Open four times and finished second four times, twice losing in play-offs. He had won the U.S. Amateur four times, and been runner-up twice. He had won the British Open three times out of the four he had entered, and he had won the British Amateur once. With the 1930 U.S. Amateur, it was thirteen major championships in eight years.

More remarkably, the championships had been won in Jones's spare time. The rest of the time he was taking a degree in mechanical engineering at Georgia Tech, a degree in literature at Harvard University, becoming a businessman, studying law, and raising a family. Unequivocally, no great golfer has ever played less formal golf than Jones.

At tournaments, local bookies listed Jones at 2 to 1. Of course, Bobby Jones didn't win all the time. It just seemed that way. Today the average touring professional golfer plays in more golf tournaments in two years than Jones did in his career. Jones played in only fifty-two tournaments; he won twenty-three of them.

Three of his most memorable victories had taken place in a span of only seven weeks, in the late spring and early summer of 1930. On two continents, in wind and cold and oppressive heat and humidity, Jones had won three major championships, one at match play and two at stroke play: respectively, the British Amateur and Open, and the United States Open.

After Jones had won the British Open, the golf writer for the *Atlanta Journal,* and Jones's thoughtful biographer, O. B. (Oscar Bane) Keeler had begun to call Jones's quest the Grand Slam, taking the phrase from the parlance of auction bridge. (George Trevor, the great sportswriter for the *New York Sun,* referred to it in terms of virgin geometrics as the "Impregnable Quadrilateral.")

In April Lloyd's of London had set the odds of Jones's winning the four major golf championships at 50 to 1. Realistically, they were 120 to 1. Unrealistically, the odds never changed, although Jones knew, as every other golfer and gambler knew, that as he annexed one championship after another, the odds of winning all four increased rather than decreased. Dozens of uncertainties loomed up like so many moated fortresses. The tiniest flaw in the Jones swing, always believed to be so controllable, suddenly could flair out of control. Jones had to bring his game to a peak four different times, which is analogous to asking the strained and exhausted marathon runner for his final kick four different times, or asking a pitcher to pitch thirty-six hitless innings.

Outwardly, Jones still appeared composed. Inwardly, he was stretching his nerves further and further, and hoping his stomach wouldn't betray him; it often did. So hard was championship golf on Jones's nervous system that during a week of competitive play, he usually lost between twelve and eighteen pounds; now and then, he fell into fits of vomiting.

Away from the fields of battle, Jones faced the ordinary matter of staying healthy from May through September 1930. Simple enough; however, strange things had been happening to him.

In June 1929, just before the U.S. Open, Jones came within a hair of being killed. One afternoon while playing a friendly round of golf with his father and two other friends at the East Lake course, a violent thunderstorm came on. As Jones was putting on the twelfth green, a lightning bolt tore into the tenth fairway, fifty feet away. The foursome raced toward the clubhouse. Just as they reached the entrance, another lightning bolt struck the chimney, showering brick and mortar 300 yards away. One piece of brick was deflected off Jones's umbrella, barely missing his head and glancing off his left shoulder, literally tearing the shirt off his back.

Then, in late July 1930, only a few weeks after Jones had won the U.S. Open, he had a second hair-raising brush with death. On his way to a business luncheon at the Town House of the Atlanta Athletic Club, he was walking down the sidewalk of Carnegie Way, a wide side street, thinking the street was deserted of traffic. It wasn't. Just as he neared the club, a voice shouted, "Look out, mister!" Jones turned and looked in horror as a runaway car was about to mount the curb less than three yards in front of him. He jumped with enough spring and power in his legs to carry him fifteen feet. Seconds later, the car crashed into the wall of the building Jones had been passing.

From September 11 until 27, Jones was under the care of two different doctors. Jones had promised to play in an exhibition on Sunday, September 14, at the East Lake course to help raise money for the first reunion in Atlanta for the United States Army's 82nd Division, which during World War I had trained outside Atlanta at Camp Gordon. The evening before the exhibition, Jones was stricken with sharp pains down the right side of the abdomen. Acute appendicitis was the first diagnosis. Jones was taken to McCrady Hospital. A second diagnosis revealed it was a severe nervous disorder for which he was given a supply of paregoric, enough to last him through the whole U.S. Amateur. A doctor agreed to accompany Jones to the Amateur.

The next day, weathering the residue of sickness, Jones went out and shot a 70, in front of 5,000 people who had paid one dollar each to see their hero. Only a few people knew that less than twenty-four hours earlier, Jones was so doubled over in pain he couldn't stand up.

Three days later, when Jones arrived at Philadelphia's Broad Street Station at 8:50 A.M., five days prior to the beginning of the U.S. Amateur, he was suffering from painful aches in his neck and shoulders. These were just occasional aches that came and went, and Jones blamed them on another round of golf he had played just the day before, a round that had ended in a downpour. Jones had played it at the Columbia Country Club in Chevy Chase, Maryland, to help raise money for the club's former assistant pro, who had been paralyzed in a car accident. Before the exhibition, Jones had been received at the White House, and President Herbert Hoover wished him the greatest success.

When Jones met the reporters the following morning, he was dressed in a light gray flannel suit and a dark gray felt hat, purposely pulled down over his pale, blue gray eyes. Jones could have passed for another commuting businessman, except he looked and felt exhausted, having boarded the train late the previous evening, and in addition was suffering from more than a mild hangover from corn whiskey.

"I'm glad to be back. Merion is a great course," he told reporters, "and I always enjoy playing it. It gives me a real thrill to return, and I hope I can win the championship. But right now I want some sleep more than anything."

So it began on a hot, hazy summer morning in Philadelphia—one of the most epic moments in all of sport. As Al Laney of the *New York Herald Tribune*, one of the finest sportswriters of the time, would later write, "The cumulative excitement of that summer-long quest, participated in by millions on both sides of the Atlantic, has no parallel in the history of sport."

Never mind that Connie Mack's Philadelphia Athletics had just won the American League pennant, or that on September 11 Bill Tilden had lost in the semi-finals of the United States singles championship at Forest Hills, his first loss to a countryman in that championship since 1919. Never mind that for the first time in five years Babe Ruth was about to lose his home-run title to Hack Wilson of the Chicago Cubs. Never mind that Sir Thomas Lipton, the famous tea merchant, had just lost in the America's Cup races for the fifth time with his yacht *Shamrock V.*

Bobby Jones was the story. He was front-page news. For the six days of the U.S. Amateur, more than 2,200,000 words were written about Jones. Radio, officially celebrating its tenth anniversary, was giving national coverage to the championship. Every evening for fifteen minutes over NBC, O. B. Keeler would report a round-up from the Merion Cricket Club. On the Wednesday before the quarter-finals, Grantland Rice with the Coca-Cola Orchestra would devote a full half hour to the U.S. Amateur.

Every public move Jones made was closely scrutinized. The editor of Philadelphia's *Evening Bulletin* assigned a total of sixteen writers and photographers just to cover the championship. One reporter's job was to follow Jones off the golf course. "I feel fine. Just fine," Jones told the reporter after he had visited an osteopath to ease the aching in his neck and shoulders.

Only in his hotel room facing Philadelphia's Schuylkill River would Jones find the peace and emotional serenity he needed. He and his entourage had checked into the Barclay Hotel on Rittenhouse Square. (The check-in had gone quietly, with Jones almost unnoticed, until a bellman dropped a sizable package with a glass container. Soon the lobby was pervaded with the odor of corn whiskey.) Jones had requested a two-bedroom suite facing west; its price was fifteen dollars per night. The suite was on one of the lower floors, for unknown to everyone but his immediate family, Jones suffered horribly from a fear of heights. There he would unwind after a day's play at Merion. As had become his custom over the years during competition, Jones's method of relaxing was simple. He soaked in a steaming hot tub while sipping a highball or two of corn whiskey.

The pressroom of the Merion Cricket Club was on the second floor of what had been the barn of a farmhouse built in 1824. In 1910 the barn was converted into a golf clubhouse. A narrow, winding staircase led to the room—an airless, musty place no more than sixty feet long and thirty feet wide with only one small window. The only things missing were rusty pitchforks and sickles. A half dozen large green-shaded lamps hung over and continually lighted a giant scoreboard nailed to a plywood wall, which served as the only divider between the pressroom and the players' locker room.

The latter was a large square room with just four windows and a grease-stained floor of wide oak planks. There were eight rows of steel-colored metal lockers fronted by long, cleat-marked benches. At either end of the room were two rickety wooden ladders, climbing high to an imaginary hayloft. Jones was given the best locker, positioned at the end of the last aisle next to a window that offered light and fresh air. He used it only for changing his shoes. Throughout the tournament, Jones wore the same pair of shoes everyday, a dark-brown-and-white handmade pair which were always kept immaculately polished and cleaned.

Much has been written about Merion, but perhaps never so poignantly as by Lee Trevino in a letter to a member of Merion's board of governors. This was after Trevino had won the 1971 U.S. Open, the thirteenth major championship played at Merion. The course then was practically unchanged from what Jones faced in the 1930 U.S. Amateur; in fact, it played twenty-one yards shorter.

"When I first saw Merion during my practice round, I will admit to a twinge of fear," wrote Trevino. "There were so many places where one could get into triple bogey position. I would have settled then and there for four par rounds. Merion was a course where *every* shot had to be played well. There could not be any lapses in concentration. It was short, by comparison, to some of the tour courses, but the narrow fairways, six-inch roughs, slick greens and 125-plus traps set in a city of trees were going to be mighty unforgiving to an error of judgement or a poorly hit shot. In brief, it struck me as a course where the player with the fewest number of misses would probably win. On another course one might miss a few times and recover. Merion was not going to let a player do that!

"Well, I got lucky and won . . . against a guy I consider to be the greatest player on the tour today—Jack Nicklaus. I didn't beat Jack by myself. I had an ally—Merion. I didn't beat Merion. I just compromised with her, like a wife, trying not to let her have her way too often."

However Jones intended to compromise with Merion, it was evident after his first practice round, Wednesday afternoon, that he was having difficulty. He shot an unspectacular three-over-par 73. He had trouble getting the feel of the greens. On the eighth green, he took ten practice putts before he sank a tricky 8-foot sidehill putt. The gallery was also troubling him. Over 4,000 people had paid one dollar each to see Jones in practice, and although the tees and greens were roped off, the fairways weren't. Marshals wearing red berets and red armbands tried to leapfrog with hand-held rope in front of the swarming gallery, but it did little good. Often the gallery packed in so thickly around Jones that he had no more than a ten-yard-wide alleyway to hit down. While Jones had played under such conditions for over a decade, he never got used to them. In fact, he was close to being terrorized by them. He constantly played in a state of fear that he would hit a stray shot that would hit and seriously injure someone. It was a miracle, given the conditions, that it never happened.

When the 1930 U.S. Amateur officially started on September 22, the problem of marshaling the gallery would be solved. For the first time in any USGA event, the armed forces were called in. Every day, fifty United States Marines in dress uniform guarded Jones.

The happiest person at Merion after Jones's first practice round was a slim nineteen-year-old with slicked-down blond hair and a narrow face named Howard Rexford. The son of a Philadelphia ink manufacturer, he was still glowing in the euphoria of having been chosen over 350 others to caddy for Jones.

The bag Rexford carried was a large oval one of leather that weighed nearly forty pounds. Rexford would carry it almost sixty miles (for which Jones paid him $175; the average caddy fee at that time was eighty-five cents a round). Jones's tools for victory consisted of eighteen clubs, not an unusual amount then. Many players carried as many as twenty to twenty-five clubs. (It wouldn't be until 1938, under the leadership of Joseph C. Dey, that the USGA would institute the fourteen-club limit.)

Two of Jones's most convincing weapons were named after women. There was his beloved putter "Calamity Jane," a small, almost toylike thing. It was a blade putter with a fragile hickory shaft around which were wrapped three bands of twine. In Jones's hands, the putter became as light as a linden leaf and more piercing than a needle's point.

Then there was his driver, "Jeanie Deans." The name fitted the club as perfectly as the club fitted the man. Jeanie Deans was the fictional heroine of Sir Walter Scott's novel, *The Heart of Midlothian*. She was a rather plain Scottish girl who possessed a strong moral earnestness and courage in refusing to lie to save her sister from hanging for a crime she didn't commit. So Jeanie Deans went to London to present her case to the Queen. The girl's character so attracted the ruler that she obtained a pardon for her sister.

Jones's other clubs carried the nomenclature of the times: spoon, baffing spoon, mid-mashie, spade mashie, mashie niblick, niblick—wonderful old Celtic names that kept people mindful of the fact that golf was a Scottish game played not only before the Industrial Revolution, but long before the American Revolution.

On Thursday morning September 18, another hot and humid day in Philadelphia, Jones took a break from practice to be made an honorary member of the exclusive Penn Athletic Club, the fifth American to be so honored (joining Colonel Clarence Chamberlain, Lieutenant Frank Schoble, Colonel Charles Lindbergh, and Rear Admiral Richard Byrd). During the presentation ceremonies, newsreels were shown of Jones winning the British Amateur, Open, and the U.S. Open. Jones sat on the small dais, dressed in a double-breasted blue suit, white shirt, and a blue-and-red-striped tie, looking more like a young diplomat than the world's greatest golfer.

Accepting the award, Jones spoke in his usual brief and lucid manner: "I certainly appreciate the honor of being enrolled in a club which has such an honored membership. I have enjoyed being here, and certainly have had an excellent time ever since I arrived in Philadelphia." More than a thousand people had jammed into the former Van Rensselaer Mansion on Walnut Street to honor Jones, and as he concluded his acceptance speech, there was a hurricane of cheering.

Such adulation would have imbued any other golfer with so much self-confidence that he would have felt he could beat par with a broomstick. For Jones, it had the opposite effect. It was another honor he felt he had to live up to.

That afternoon, in his second practice round, Jones barely broke 80, shooting a sloppy 78. He was angry, and at times almost threw his clubs to his caddy. His frustration had been compounded by a gallery of 4,000-plus, a crowd so dense and close as to not let him hit even one extra practice shot.

Joining the massive human fringe surrounding Jones as he played the last two holes was Jess Sweetser, himself very much a contestant. Sweetser had won the 1922 U.S. Amateur, and in 1926 he had become the first American-born golfer to win the British Amateur. By 1930 he was ranked as one of the top four amateurs in the country. Sweetser thought he had the answer to Jones's problem, and that night he called Jones.

"Hey, Bob, I see you've begun throwing your clubs again."

"Goddamnit, who the hell is this? Sweets?" roared Jones.

"Look, Bob," Sweetser said, "you know Merion. Christ, you've probably played it thirty times. What you need is to get away from the crowds. Relax. Get in some practice. Let's go down to Pine Valley tomorrow. There'll be no gallery and no reporters."

Jones agreed. But even at Pine Valley Golf Club in the nearby hinterland of Clementon, New Jersey, Jones attracted a crowd. Six of the club's caddies followed Jones, as did a reporter for the *Evening Bulletin*, who wrote that Jones had cursed madly at some squawking ducks in a pond while putting on the fourteenth green.

On the first nine holes, Jones picked up his ball three times, suffering, to some degree, the plight of many an average golfer who has played Pine Valley. Its fairways and greens literally are islands of green lawns surrounded by oceans of unraked sand. It is the epitome of target golf. Each drive must reach the fairway; each approach must reach the green. There are easier courses—in fact, almost any—on which to play one's game into shape and steady one's confidence.

Jones was trying to accomplish both. He kept running into patches of mediocre golf, and was baffled until he came to the ninth hole, a long straight par 4 with a two-acre fairway surrounded by sand. Jones's drive found the middle of the fairway, and then he laced a spade-mashie shot five feet from the pin and holed the putt. Feeling like the halfback who, having been unable to get beyond the line of scrimmage all day, finally cuts into the open, Jones was off. He played the next nine holes brilliantly with seven pars and two birdies for a 33.

A somewhat more relaxed and confident Jones, an ardent baseball fan (a vice president of the Atlanta Crackers), then spent the afternoon with Sweetser at the ballpark in Philadelphia, watching the National League leaders, the St. Louis Cardinals, beat the hometown Phillies.

The following day, as more than 5,000 spectators followed Jones, he shot a 74; however, the main topic of conversation was his health, not his golf. He looked wan. That morning he had been seized with fits of vomiting. "I feel fine, really," he told reporters. "I just ate too much Brunswick Stew last night." More denials and controversies would follow.

On Sunday, the day before the two qualifying rounds, Jones broke his usual routine in preparing for a championship. Instead of reading in his hotel room or going fishing to relieve his anxiety, Jones played another practice round. Finley Douglas, president of the USGA, and Robert Lesley, president of Merion Cricket Club—aware of the thousands and thousands of dollars Jones was generating every day he stepped on the golf course—had approached him and hesitantly asked if he really wouldn't mind too much playing just one more practice round.

It was a lot to ask of a man, but Jones reluctantly agreed. This taxing of his privacy was just one of the many prices he had learned to pay for fame. To put Jones's drawing power in perspective, one should understand that for the six days of the 1930 U.S. Amateur, during the Depression, the total receipts were $55,319. By contrast, the gross receipts of the 1964 U.S. Amateur were $17,261.

Jones teed off just past 11:00 A.M. Sunday morning. His father was with him, having just arrived that morning from Atlanta, where at that very moment Jones's wife, Mary, four months pregnant with her third child, was at Mass praying for her husband to win and finally get it over with. She was hoping this would be the end.

Jones's game began to peak that Sunday. He shot a one-under-par 69 and made up for the fifty-four holes he had played at Merion without a birdie by scoring four birdies. He was more satisfied with his game, and his mood turned expansive. During the round, while walking down the seventh fairway, he was joined by his friend, and the most famous sportswriter of the time, Grantland Rice.

"Granny," Jones said, "I've suffered at this game a lot of years. Among other things, I've discovered a man must play golf by 'feel' . . . the hardest thing in the world to describe—but the easiest thing in the world to sense when you have it completely. . . . Today I have it completely. I don't have to think of anything . . . just meet the ball. But during championships, I've had to rivet on one, two and sometimes three checkpoints in my mind, usually on each shot. Hell, there are a hundred checkpoints if you want to be technical, but I find I can hold onto no more than three at the most and still meet the ball."

"And what are your three checks, Bob?" Rice asked.

"Dragging . . . rather than lifting that clubhead back, bringing my left hip into action at the start of my downswing and keeping my left arm close to my body—from inside out—for the completion of the shot. Today everything is falling into one piece—perfect. But it seldom happens—at least with me—and very seldom in title play."

2

To understand the source of energy of the Joneses, one begins in Canton, Georgia, with Bobby Jones's grandfather, Robert Tyre Jones, Sr. He was a huge man for his time, almost six feet five inches tall, weighing 235 pounds. His most prominent and inherited feature was his brawn—an immense back, shoulders, and chest. His jacket size was forty-eight; his waist was forty. He had a ruddy complexion, short, nut-brown hair, and a large open face with deep-set brown eyes that usually stared at you from behind rimless spectacles. When angered, he had a look that could send a coiled rattlesnake slithering into the bush. He was a rigid disciplinarian with an austere manner and a deep, gravelly voice that rarely sounded with gaiety. He had no comprehension of games and looked upon all sports as a waste of time.

Robert Tyre Jones, Sr., didn't swear, smoke, or drink, not even Coca-Cola. He considered card playing sinful. Every Sunday for more than fifty years, he attended the 9:30 Sunday school and worship services at the First Baptist Church of Canton. While the ministers preached the faith, Robert Tyre Jones was the faith.

While Sunday was for him a day of worship, a day of rest and not of play, he was always telling his grandson, "Bob, if you have to play golf on Sunday, play well." The words were not casually proffered, but rather held the tone of an edict to a criminal on parole. Even when his own children were growing up in Canton, if they wanted to play on Sunday, it always was after church, and then they had to sneak away from the house. One Sunday when it was inevitable that he work, a colleague mistakenly joked to him, "Well, R. T. [as he was called], I guess there's no rest for the wicked." Jones humorlessly snapped back, "And the righteous don't need it."

Born in 1849, and too young to fight in the Civil War, R. T. Jones worked the war-ravaged land of the family farm near Covington, Georgia, until he was thirty. Then with his wife, his six-month-old son, and $500, he moved to Canton in the foothills of the Blue Ridge Mountains, nestled in the sweeping bend of the Etowah River.

The year was 1879, when R. T. Jones established the Jones Mercantile Company. His first week's business consisted of one transaction—swapping a pound of nails for a pair of hand-knitted socks. But R. T. Jones wouldn't be denied his fortune. His recreation was his work, and his work was his way of serving the Lord. His interpretation of "The Lord is my Shepherd . . ." was literal.

By 1890 the Jones Mercantile Company netted $50,000. Ten years later, despite the 1893 Depression, profits exceeded $100,000. On December 2, 1899, at the age of fifty, Jones started the Canton Cotton Mills. The first year, the mill lost 10 percent of its capital investment. Ninety percent of the stockholders were from the local county, and at the first annual stockholders' meeting Jones offered to buy whatever stock they wished to sell. He then outlined plans for expansion, saying, "I'm not used to running a business at a loss."

He took over the operation of the business himself and went into manufacturing denim. In 1903 the firm netted $400,000. By 1925 earnings were over $1,500,000.

R. T. Jones believed in the South, its land, its people, hard work, and God. He was a man who personified what was beginning to be known in the South during the 1880s and the 1890s as the "New South," as expressed by a brilliant Atlanta journalist and orator named Henry W. Grady. Addressing the New England Society in New York City on the evening of December 21, 1886, Grady told his audience, "The old South rested everything on slavery and agriculture, unconscious that these could neither give nor maintain healthy growth. The new South presents a perfect democracy, the oligarchs leading in the popular movement—a social system compact and closely knit, less splendid on the surface, but stronger at the core—a hundred farms for every plantation, fifty homes for every palace—and a diversified industry that meets the complex needs of this complex age.

"The new South is enamored of her new work. Her Soul is stirred with the breath of a new life. The light of grandeur is falling fair on her face. She is thrilling to the consciousness of growing power and prosperity. As she stands upright, full-statured and equal among the people of the earth, breathing the keen air and looking out upon the expanded horizon, she understands that her emancipation came because through the inscrutable wisdom of God her honest purpose was crossed, and her brave armies were beaten.

"This is said in no spirit of time-saving or apology. The South has nothing to take back . . ."

In September 1937, R. T. Jones died only one month prior to his eighty-eighth birthday. He was a rich man, with a personal fortune valued in excess of $5 million. The inheritors were many. R. T. Jones believed in a family work force. By two wives he had fathered fourteen children, of which eleven lived to maturity. Collectively, by 1937, his children had given him twenty-seven grandchildren.

His eldest offspring was Robert Purmedus Jones, born in 1879. He was an easy-going child, a joiner more by nature than necessity, and a lover of most games and sports. Never in need of a playmate, he was always ready for play, quite the opposite from his father. He also rebelled against his father's suppressed nature with a stormy and vocal temper. Before he was a teenager, he had acquired an extensive swearing vocabulary which would become one of his lifetime trademarks. Although he was six inches shorter than his father, Robert did inherit the Jones brawn and was naturally gifted with excellent coordination.

His sport was baseball, and he could play. He so excelled at the game that for three years at Mercer University in Macon—1896 to 1898—he played first-string varsity. He also played first string for one year, 1899, at the University of Georgia in Athens, where he received his Bachelor of Laws degree. He was such an outstanding first baseman and hitter, consistently batting over .300, that he was offered a baseball contract with a National League team called the Brooklyn Superbas (earlier called the Brooklyn Trolley Dodgers, later the Brooklyn Dodgers).

The Triumph

When Jones told his father about the baseball contract, the response was typical of R. T. Jones: "I didn't send you to college to become a professional baseball player." And that was that. It was a severe disappointment to Robert, although perhaps not unexpected. R. T. Jones was a difficult man to please. His father never had seen his son play even one game of baseball, and if a young man ever needed his father's approval for his athletic prowess, it was Robert.

But Robert's most profound disappointment, which would forever weigh on his own sense of self-worth, was that as the eldest child of an old southern family he had not been given the full family name to carry on. When his own second son was born, he christened him Robert Tyre Jones, and when the boy was eleven, and his name began to appear in the papers, he added Junior to the name. What more could he do to please his father? Bobby Jones kept the Junior simply because it made his own father happy.

In June 1899, Robert P. Jones was admitted to the Georgia bar, and in September that year he set up practice in Atlanta. Financially, it was rough going, and in less than a year he returned to Canton and joined his father in business. On June 1, 1900, in Auburn, Alabama, at age twenty-one, he married Clara Merrick Thomas.

Clara was a shy, sometimes reclusive girl, unsentimental and devoid of any moony-romantic side. Basically empirical, she was naturally drawn to the gregarious and sportive attorney. She saw in him the strong threads she would help weave into the fabric of his financial success.

It was a good thing that Robert P. Jones had a capacity to earn a handsome living, for Clara Jones was an expensive wife who had grown up conscious of social rank and privilege. Her father, William Bailey, had served as a captain in the Spanish-

American War and was one of the most prominent judges in Auburn. Clara and her younger sister were raised in a huge Greek Revival house in the then very fashionable northeast side of Auburn. She was her father's favorite child, and the bond of father/daughter attachment was always firmly sealed. For her sixteenth birthday, he gave her a pair of Paris-made shoes with eight-inch heels. From then on, whatever the fashion, she would wear no other type shoe.

Intellectually, Clara was a quick learner with a wonderfully intelligent curiosity, a trait she passed on to her son. In the spring of 1899 she was presented at the Auburn Debutante Cotillion Ball, and later that spring completed high school. Her grades were so high she could have gone to almost any woman's college, but instead, that fall, she accompanied her father on a long business trip to Atlanta, where she met Robert P. Jones.

Physically, Clara was a wisp of a woman, with thin legs, a tiny waist, and a small bosom. She stood exactly five feet tall, weighed just over ninety pounds, and looked frail. Her small oval face was pretty with stark features and a bone structure seemingly as delicate as porcelain. She had a sensuous full mouth and large, warm gray eyes. Her hands were doll-like in size, though she kept her fingernails scratchably long. Her laugh was spontaneous, high-pitched, like the tinkling of small silver bells. In all, she exuded a rather vampish nature. Nothing could have been further from the truth.

She had no patience for scheming or being wily, and she considered gossip frivolous. Her manner was quick, direct, open, and often opinionated. When her husband had one too many highballs at a party and started playing the piano and singing in a deep bass voice, Clara would abruptly say, "Big

Bob, sit down and shut up." There was nothing inhibited about Clara.

From her husband, she learned to swear. During World War II she damned with equal fervor President Franklin Roosevelt, Prime Minister Winston Churchill, and columnist Walter Lippman. When it came to the Japanese, it wasn't any one individual that infuriated her, but the whole nation. In the 1950s, she was heard to say, "Goddamn them, as if Pearl Harbor wasn't bad enough, now they've gone and gotten into the textile market."

While Big Bob was the likable dancing bear, Clara Jones you either liked or you didn't.

In April 1901, in Canton, Clara gave birth to her first child, a boy. She named him after her beloved father, William Bailey. The baby was small, just over five pounds, and had trouble gaining weight. He also lacked the normal infantile immunities against disease. After three months, the baby contracted pneumonia and died on July 10, 1901. He was buried in the family plot in Canton, and his name was never mentioned again. Thereafter, Clara referred to him "as the baby that died."

The death shook Clara's deepest emotional roots. If Canton had had a hospital, better doctors, she told Robert, her baby might have been saved. Shortly after William Bailey was buried, Clara became pregnant again, and upon her urging, they moved to Atlanta. It was the second best move they made.

At 7:35 A.M. on March 17, 1902, a mild day in Atlanta, Clara Jones gave birth, at home on Willow Street, to another boy. He was named after Robert's father. The baby, Bobby Jones, weighed just over five pounds, and like the first was very frail.

3

Besides the fact that Bobby Jones was born in 1902, there were other reasons the year was a good one for golf. The rubber-core golf ball—the one presently in use—was legalized in 1902, adding at least twenty yards to drives. The 1902 U.S. Open was won by professional Laurie Auchertlonie, who collected $200 and, using the new ball, became the first golfer to break 80 for four Open rounds.

In 1902 the top sportswriter for the *Atlanta Journal*, on salary for $12.50 per week, was a twenty-two-year-old Greek and Latin Phi Beta Kappa graduate of Vanderbilt University by the name of Henry Grantland Rice. This was a Victorian time in America, when sports and play were believed to be for boys and fools, and Rice helped to break down the barrier. While he was the great evangelist of fun, the unabashed romantic about sports and their players, always the bringer of good news about games, more importantly, he put the playing fields on a different plane by making them respectable. With its dancing metaphors, his prose leaped from the sports pages and ignited a whole nation with its fanciful and often alliterative sobriquets for sporting heroes. Rice was the first to call Ty Cobb "the Georgia Peach," Red Grange "the Galloping Ghost," and Jack Dempsey "the Manassa Mauler." Perhaps his most inspired appellation occurred in late October 1924 at the Notre Dame–Army football game played at the Polo Grounds in the Bronx, New York, when he named the Notre Dame backfield "the Four Horsemen." (Today, even the most prolific sportswriter pales next to Rice. In a career that spanned over half a century, Rice's output, usually under the pressure of a deadline, was prodigious. He wrote over 1,000 magazine articles, 7,000 words of verse—he never called one a poem—22,000 columns, and hundreds of movie scripts for a total of 67 million words, or what would amount to 670 average-length books. Until he died at age seventy-three, quite appropriately and relatively painlessly of a heart attack at his typewriter, he was turning out a syndicated column six days a week.

Bobby Jones was a sickly child, almost as vulnerable to infantile diseases as his late brother. He was allergic to most solid foods and milk, and was terribly colicky. Contrary to the pediatric rule of thumb, he didn't even come close to tripling his birth weight in his first year. Robert and Clara took him from one pediatrician to another, a half dozen in all. The diagnosis was always the same: the boy probably wouldn't survive infancy. Every day that Bobby Jones lived was a triumph. At the age of three, he was able to keep down just three things: egg whites, pabulum, and black-eyed peas.

Most of the daily care and feeding of the infant was the responsibility of a kindly black nursemaid named Camilla. She was a young, heavyset woman, good-natured and with a natu-

ral child-rearing gift. She dispensed discipline with equal por-
tions of praise, which wasn't easy with a housebound infant.
Over and over again, Camilla read Bobby the *Tales of Uncle
Remus*, authored by Atlantan Joel Chandler Harris. In time
there was hardly an episode between Br'er Rabbit and Br'er
Fox that Bobby didn't know almost word for word. Like so
many youngsters whose minds can grasp a good story, Bobby
would interrupt and correct Camilla whenever she would leave
out even a word, making her go back and reread the sentence.
Only when the weather was perfect would Clara allow Bobby
outside to ride his tricycle around the backyard.

Bobby's father instituted the boy's only chore. It was to
keep the Jones's pet dog, a black-and-white collie named
Judge, at home. A friendly dog, Judge was apt to follow anyone leaving the house. With Bobby on the alert, Judge never
got more than a block away.

While he was mainly cared for by Camilla, Bobby was also
strictly watched over and guided by Clara Jones, now a very
nervous and overprotective mother. She wasn't about to lose
another child. At twenty-three, Clara appeared fragile; in reality she was about as fragile as steel wire. She remained just one
step out of the light of being her son's shadow. It was Clara
who strummed the tune of his infancy.

Both parents were almost maniacally fearful that other children might infect their child, and while Bobby was rarely
in want of attention, he keenly felt the deprivation of the
healthy stimulus of contemporary playmates. For more than
five years, Bobby Jones was a prisoner of his parents' fears.

It was no wonder that when Little Bob—as Bobby was
called for a brief time, until he put a stop to it—became interested in golf, his parents were delighted and supportive. While
golf is one of the world's oldest and most sophisticated games,

it is also a highly individualistic one—a noncontact sport essentially played in a clean environment.

Despite the seemingly ideal conditions of golf, the wounds of Bobby Jones's infancy were deep. He remained shy, a very private, introverted, and reserved person. All his life he felt uneasy in crowds, especially when he was the center of attention. He often stated that he never felt quite so alone as when on a fairway or green surrounded by thousands and thousands of admirers. He detested having to shake hands with every stranger who wanted to touch the one and only Bobby Jones. He hated being a celebrity.

Whenever Bobby Jones did discover friendship, it was like other people discovering a sunken treasure. His capacity for friendship was enormous, and he always had the emotional energy to fuel that relationship. He loved his friends; they were family to him, and few human beings have put themselves through more punishment for their friends than Jones. Once he began winning golf tournaments, his friends would wager sizable sums of money on him. When Jones became aware of this, of just how much his winning meant to his friends in affection and pride, he truly began to suffer.

Bobby Jones discovered golf and friendship simultaneously.

It was the summer of 1907, when Little Bob was almost five and a half years old and vacationing with his parents in the sporting community of East Lake. Though it was only five miles east of Atlanta's city limits, East Lake was then very much in the country. The Joneses took over part of a large boarding house along the second fairway of the East Lake golf course of the Atlanta Athletic Club.

Golf was still a rather exclusive game in the United States in 1907. Less than 100,000 people played it. Golf clubs had been started in the 1700s in Georgia, South Carolina, and New

York, but for the most part they had been founded by Scots homesick for the game and their country. None lasted long. It wasn't until 1888, when a transplanted Scot named John Reid founded the St. Andrews Golf Club in Yonkers, New York, that golf truly began to flourish. Reid's timing, though accidental, was impeccable.

Already, country clubs—molded more after the estates of England, with their aristocratic weekend recreations, than after the spartan English hunt and golf clubs—had been started around Boston. Two of the first were the Myopia Hunt Club in Winchester and The Country Club in Brookline (the latter remains the oldest existing country club in the United States), but both clubs were centered around horse racing, hunting, and overall family activities rather than golf. What the country club really needed was a sport for men and women of all ages, something for which one didn't have to be young, quick, or extraordinarily coordinated to play reasonably well. Golf answered these needs, and much more, for at the heart of the game's popularity rests its eternal hope for improvement.

The East Lake course, opened in 1901, was Atlanta's first. In its original design (in 1914, it was redesigned), it was rather unorthodox. It began with a medium-length par 3, followed by a par 5, and then another par 3. The next fifteen holes consisted of long par 4s. It was an incredibly difficult course to score on. Besides golf, the Atlanta Athletic Club had a lake for swimming, boating and fishing, stables for horses, and tennis courts.

Although Atlanta's golfing population then was small, it did encompass some of the city's most prominent citizens, including a corps of Coca-Cola executives. Robert P. Jones had just taken on a new law partner and was beginning to do contractual legal work between the Coca-Cola Company and the bottling companies. With his natural love of games, he began to take up golf in the summer of 1907, and Clara, with her inherent curiosity and her social awareness, also began. Little Bob wasn't even allowed on the course, but for the first time in his young life, he was free to play outside.

He made the most of his freedom. Next to the house he discovered a raspberry patch; to a youngster used to a bland diet, raspberries were ambrosia. Bobby played baseball, tennis and fished. He also rode on an old donkey, which walked very slowly, despite his prodding, and always left the stables in the same direction and would go for no more than a block or two. In his childish anger, the boy named the donkey Clara.

The son of the owner of the boarding house was a seven-year-old named Frank Meador. Bigger and older than Bobby, he was told by his parents to sort of keep an eye on the frail little boarder. If Frank Meador knew he was to be a conduit for history, he couldn't possibly have done things better. Already he had become intrigued in trying to hit a small stationary ball with a club. He encouraged Little Bob, who took to his first friend and his friend's pastime with a compulsion to please and a fear of making a fool of himself.

Since neither of the boys was allowed on the East Lake golf course, they laid out their own little course, consisting of two holes, each a little more than 100 yards long. The first hole ran along the roadway in front of the boarding house, and the other across the road and back along a wide ditch. There were no greens, and the cups consisted of large gouged-out holes. One of the older men boarders found a discarded club and cut it down to fit Bobby. It was a cleek, quite similar to the present-day 2-iron, not the easiest club with which to learn to hit a golf ball. Not surprisingly, when Jones became a great player, one of the strongest parts of his game was his long-iron game.

At age five and a half, however, Little Bob harbored no such dreams of greatness. He was too busy dancing madly in the street whenever he sliced or shanked a ball into a brier patch. It was a ludicrous sight, the little tow-headed boy, weighing no more than forty pounds, dressed in a cotton sunsuit with short pants, hopping up and down in the middle of a dirt road shaking a golf club and cursing. Even at that young age, inside that little body was a giant, wild temper. He would learn slowly and painfully to check it.

Bobby Jones learned two things about golf from that first summer in 1907: he learned to play the ball as it lies, whether in the road, on a grassy patch, or in the ditch; and he learned that it is easier to lose golf balls than to find them. The price of a golf ball in 1907 was twenty cents.

Surprisingly, he didn't experience any sudden surge of passion for the game, even when he hit a good shot. It was all rather incidental. Bobby Jones would rather have been playing baseball, but because of the dearth of boys around the suburb of East Lake, there were never enough boys to make up two even abbreviated teams.

The next summer the Joneses moved permanently to East Lake, to a house inside the club grounds just off the thirteenth green. It was the best move they ever made. Little Bob now was allowed on the course, to tag along with his mother and father, provided he would take only one club and could keep up. It didn't work. Finally, the boy was given two additional clubs, a cut-down brassie from his mother and a cut-down mashie from his father: these, with his faithful cleek, comprised his first set. He kept up fairly well, walking quickly between shots, simply beating the ball along.

It was a good year for the youngster. Though still spindly, he was gaining weight and becoming more and more active, enough to make his mother more and more nervous. It was the year when the luckiest thing in golf happened to him.

As at all golf and country clubs of the time, a large measure of social status was gained by employing a Scottish golf pro, the more Scotch the better. It was not unusual for Scots who had been in the United States for many years, and played a good game of golf, simply to thicken their brogues and gain immediate employment as golf pros. For three years, Atlanta Athletic Club's pro was Jimmy Maiden from Carnoustie, Scotland.

Jimmy was leaving the club for another club in the summer of 1908, and his position was being taken over by his brother Stewart. The first time Little Bob met Stewart, the boy was with his parents. They talked at length to Stewart, who simply nodded occasionally. Bobby's first impression of him was that he couldn't talk at all. When Stewart finally did say a few words, Little Bob couldn't understand them, so thick was the man's brogue. Literally, Stewart was just off the boat.

He was a small man with a pinched face, a squinty look around his eyes, and a high seamy forehead. His shoulders and arms were as thick and strong as a blacksmith's. He liked good and bad whiskey equally, and there usually was a cigarette dangling from his lips.

His main characteristic was frugality. He was as tight with a dollar as he was economical with words. He could be presented with the most complex theory of the golf swing and summarize it in a few syllables. With little effort, Stewart Maiden could have invented the declarative sentence.

Almost twenty years after that first meeting, Bobby Jones had occasion to profit from Stewart Maiden's concise language. The 1927 U.S. Open was played at the Oakmont Country Club, a course noted equally for its large, slick greens and its 200-plus furrowed bunkers. Jones became intimidated by the bunkers. He played his worst Open, finishing tied for eleventh. An angered and frustrated Jones returned to Atlanta and sought Maiden's advice. Off they went to the practice tee. Stewart watched as Jones sliced one drive and then hooked the next. On and on it went for five minutes. Finally Stewart said, "Bob, hit the hell out of the ball."

Jones did just that. The ball sailed long and straight. He hit another, another, and another, all with the same results. He turned to thank Stewart, but already Stewart was walking back to the pro shop. To Stewart, the problem was simple: Jones was trying to steer the ball. The man's method of teaching was always direct and terse. He never tried to make over a swing, and he avoided getting into a discussion on the theory of the golf swing. Simply, his eye went to the pupil's basic problem, which if corrected would improve the performance of the whole swing.

Maiden's own swing was fairly upright and smooth with a full pivot, and rather wristy. His manner of play was characteristic of the man. He wasted little time. He simply walked up to the ball, took his stance, and hit it.

At six and a half, Bobby Jones thought Stewart's way of swinging and playing was the best at the club, and he began to tag along whenever the pro played. But Stewart didn't pay the slightest attention to the youngster, and after four or five holes Bobby would leave, go home, get some balls, and practice pitching to the thirteenth green, trying to imitate Stewart in his mind's eye. Fortunately, Bobby Jones was not just a good mimic, he was a great one. To the finest detail, Jones copied Maiden's swing. By the time he reached his teens, he was often mistaken for Maiden. As Jones matured and grew, his swing became more upright, and his stance narrowed to facilitate an almost ninety degree hip turn; but the haste with which he played and complete lack of any extraneous movement were Maiden's. Thus, from the beginning, Jones was a very fast player. Partnered with another good player, Jones's average time around East Lake was two and a half hours.

He was also a very nervous player. While he never learned to completely harness his temper, he did learn to harness his nerves. Bernard Darwin once wrote about Jones, ". . . there is no one so formidable as the nervous player who can control his nerves."

Bobby Jones was six when he played in his first tournament. It was a six-hole event, a sort of makeshift junior, junior championship of the club for youngsters between the ages of six and ten. The tournament was organized by the Meadors, the owners of the boarding house, and its entrants consisted of four youngsters. And what a foursome it was. There was Bob, his friend Frank, and another new playmate, Perry Adair, three and a half years Bobby's senior. Perry would become a first-class golfer in his own right, the original "Dixie Boy Wonder."

The other member of the foursome, four years older than Bob, was a beautiful girl with blazing red hair. Her name was Alexa Stirling, and she would win the Women's National Amateur three consecutive years—1916, 1919, and 1920 (the championship was cancelled during 1917 and 1918)—and be runner-up three other times. Alexa was more than a golf champion, she was a champion of fair play.

Against the three boys, she asked no quarter and gave none as she beat them. But the organizers of the tournament felt they just couldn't have a girl beating three boys, so they declared Bobby Jones the winner and awarded him the three-inch-high sterling silver cup. Alexa didn't complain. Her be-wildered friend accepted the trophy and slept with it under his pillow that night.

Three years later, Bobby won the club's junior champion-ship legitimately, beating a boy seven years his senior. By now Little Bob was scoring consistently in the low 90s. Two years later he sank a 4-foot putt on the final green for an 80. The next year his scores began to dip into the 70s. His father was still playing in the high 80s and taking the game very seriously. He was also taking his son's game very seriously, being con-stantly present for approval and encouragement. He remem-bered that his own father had never watched him play even one game of baseball, and he tended to overcompensate with his own son. A bear hug was often an expression of Big Bob's sublimation, but that was all right. Big Bob could be ex-cused for being something of a stage father pushing his son, standing in the wings vicariously enjoying his son's success. He probably would have been a very good professional baseball player.

He told his son that when he was fifteen and good enough, he could enter the Southern Amateur, one of the South's big-gest tournaments. Bobby was then twelve, at the very top of boyhood, and fifteen seemed a decade away. But the next year, with Bobby only thirteen, the tournament was to be played at East Lake, and Big Bob relented and entered his son.

Bobby made it to the finals of the second flight. He was by then five feet two inches tall, a stocky boy with a fierce temper and competitive drive. To get to the finals, he had to beat three men, all twice his age, with the smallest standing six feet three inches tall and weighing over 200 pounds. He lost in the finals 2 and 1, shooting an approximate 78.

1. Bobby Jones at age seven, still a rather frail child who would much rather have been playing baseball than golf.

2. At age fourteen, Bobby Jones competes in his first major championship, the 1916 U.S. Amateur at the Merion Cricket Club. He is still the youngest golfer ever to reach the quarter-finals of that championship.

3. Stewart Maiden, often called "Kiltie the King Maker," after whom Jones modeled his swing and from whom he very occasionally received a lesson.

4. Two of the Dixie Whiz Kids: Jones (lower right) and Perry Adair (upper right). Stewart Maiden sits next to Jones, with Frank Meacock (upper left).

5. Alexa Stirling of Atlanta, one of Jones's first competitors and winner of the U.S. Women's Amateur 1916, 1919, and 1920.

6. Jones, during his first year at Harvard University, practices for the 1923 U.S. Open. Unable to play on Harvard's golf team because he had already played for Georgia Tech, Jones accepted the humble position of team assistant manager. Two months after this picture was taken, Jones won his first of four U.S. Opens and first of thirteen major championships.

He brooded and moped about his loss. At thirteen, Bobby Jones thought he should have won the Southern Amateur, that he really hadn't won anything yet, only a few junior tournaments. As far as he was concerned he had disgraced his family, Stewart Maiden, the Atlanta Athletic Club, and his high school. He was living by standards that men twice and three times his age could not have maintained.

The boy's overbearing ambition was typical of a city hungering for recognition as one of the South's central capitals. In 1910 the population of Atlanta was 154,839. Over the previous decade it had increased over 30 percent. The Coca-Cola Company was pleased to promote the fact that 3 million glasses of Coke were being drunk each day.

By 1915 Atlanta was a major annual stop for the Metropolitan Opera. Begun in 1910 at the suggestion of the opera singer Geraldine Farrar, the tour had been a bold venture for a small city. Even the most optimistic officers of the Met had doubted its success, for the company required a guarantee of $40,000. The money for that first tour was raised in less than a week by 200 culture-hungry Atlantans. The Met gave six performances, to a total attendance of 27,000 people, producing gross receipts of $72,030. The Met's General Director Giulio Gatti-Casazza said, "Never before had the Metropolitan Opera Company sung to so many people or earned such an amount of money in one week, despite the fact that six or more performances are given in a week in New York."

The opera was one of the features of Atlanta's spring social season, and Clara Jones was one of the patrons of the opera. She tried to interest her husband, but Big Bob would have none of it, so slowly and carefully Clara introduced her son to opera and classical music. It took. The same person who could be so fidgety and anxious on the golf course to get to the next shot, and who afterward in the locker room with a towel draped around his middle would stand arm in arm with his dad singing "Home on the Range," had this other side. He could sit for hours listening to opera, and in the privacy of his own home, he would sing arias from operas by Wagner, Verdi, and Puccini.

Also part of Atlanta's great pride was the competitive spirit of the Georgia Tech football coach, John Heisman (for whom the trophy is named). In his sixteen years at Tech, Heisman never had a losing season. From 1915 to 1918, his team won the Southern Intercollegiate Athletic Association, and he was the first of three Tech coaches to win over 100 games. His overall record was an enviable one, 102–29–7. Every fall on the first day of practice, Heisman would greet his squad, hold up a football, and say, "What is it? It is a prolate spheroid—that is, an elongated sphere—in which the outer leathern casing is drawn tightly over a somewhat smaller rubber tubing. Better to have died as a small boy than any of you to fumble it."

Caught up in the spirit of the times, Bobby Jones played in a rush of tournaments in 1916. His father entered him in almost every significant invitational event in the South. If his son didn't win, Big Bob certainly was not going to deny him the chance to try. Little Bob won three invitationals, plus the East Lake club championship. Now he was consistently scoring in the low 70s. He won one tournament with a final round of three under par, a 69.

Even then, he could make the game look so easy. It was no wonder he took his genius for granted. He figured if he couldn't outdrive an opponent, he could make up the slack by sticking a pitch shot next to the pin. (And if he didn't hole every 15-foot putt, he could get as mad as if he were still six years old and had just sliced a ball into a brier patch.)

The first Georgia State Amateur was played in 1916 over the Brookhaven course of Atlanta's Capital City Club. In the thirty-six-hole match-play finals, it was Bobby Jones against his friendly rival—the "Dixie Boy Wonder," Perry Adair.

At the end of the first eighteen holes, Jones was 3 down and having putting problems. After lunch, he went to practice on his putting. He had been at it for about five minutes when the chairman of the tournament, Ralph Reed, approached him. Since several hundred people had arrived for the afternoon round, Reed asked if he would mind playing out the bye-holes—implying that Adair would beat him.

The words had the same effect on Jones as the sting of a whip against the flank of a thoroughbred horse three furlongs behind in a race. Jones's face flushed red with anger. His eyes turned a steel gray. He snapped back, "Mr. Reed, don't worry, there won't be any bye-holes!"

On the very first hole of the afternoon round, Jones shoved his second shot into the woods and took a double bogey 6. Now he was 4 down. Over the next seventeen holes—for the first time conscious of the incredible strain of tournament golf—Jones played brilliantly. He never was over par. He made fifteen pars and two birdies, beating Adair on the final green.

Such was the caliber of play by both Jones and Adair that Reed, a committeeman for the USGA, determined both were good enough to go to the Merion Cricket Club in Ardmore, Pennsylvania, to play in the U.S. Amateur. At that time to play in the championship a golfer had to have a handicap of six or under and be approved by the USGA. The entry fee was five dollars.

It was the first time Jones had been north of the Mason-Dixon Line, and the first time he had putted on fast, bent grass greens. During one practice round, he misread the speed of a putt so badly that the ball rolled off the green and into a brook. Nonetheless, Bobby Jones was cocky, not the slightest bit intimidated by the fact that he was in a strange area, playing a strange course, that among his opponents would be seasoned competitors twice and three times his age, and that his chances of even qualifying were about 1 in 5 (only 32 players would qualify out of a field of 157). Was anyone in championship competition ever so innocent?

And he looked it, even though he had grown two inches in the last year. He had by now a voracious appetite; his lunch or dinner wasn't complete without two or three extra helpings of ice cream. He was beginning to take on the Joneses' brawn. His wheat-colored hair was parted down the left side. His face was full and freckled. He wore a white shirt with a starched collar and a bow tie. His trousers—the only pair he had bothered to bring with him—were a light brown wool. His golf shoes were high-topped old army shoes to which he had added spikes.

To many of the players and spectators, Jones appeared rather hayseed, very much out of his league. Those who thought so only had to wait for the qualifying rounds. These consisted of thirty-six holes of stroke play, eighteen played over Merion's easier West Course, an uninspired layout with only 12 bunkers, and eighteen over the East Course, the site of the championship with its 125-plus bunkers. At match play, the first round would be eighteen holes with all other matches at thirty-six holes.

Jones surprised everyone but himself when, in the morning qualifying round, he whipped around the West Course in 74 and led all qualifiers. After lunch Jones got one of the biggest surprises of his young life. Surrounding the first tee were over a thousand people. As at any tournament, the gallery follows a major player, a leading contender, or a new phenomenon.

Jones was the latter. Word had spread that "the Kid from Dixie" was breaking up the tournament.

Already uncomfortable in crowds, Jones suddenly was seized with a case of stage fright. His swing tightened. He sprayed shots. Putts refused to drop. From a 74, he rocketed to an 89, but his total of 163 qualified him for the championship. When his friend Perry Adair also qualified, the two youngsters hugged each other and danced up and down in front of the scoreboard.

The pool of qualifiers was deep in talent, as impressive—if not more so—than that of any contemporary Amateur championship. There was a U.S. Open champion and three former U.S. Amateur champions. Besides Jones, there were five state champions with a collective total of eleven state amateur championships. There were also two NCAA champions and an equal number of North and South Amateur winners.

Jones's first opponent was Eben Byers, winner of the 1906 U.S. Amateur and a veteran of sixteen U.S. Amateurs. He stood only a half inch taller than Jones, but was twenty-two years his senior.

It was an unusual match, one of the youngest players against one of the oldest; yet both expressed their exasperation over a missed shot the same way, by throwing their club. It almost became a contest of who could throw his club the farthest. The players behind them later said it looked like a juggling act on stage. At the twelfth hole, Byers got so furious at a missed shot he threw his club over a hedge and refused to let his caddy retrieve it. Jones won the match 3 and 2. Years later he recalled whimsically that he had won only because Byers had run out of clubs first. Byers took the defeat hard and never again qualified for the U.S. Amateur.

Next Jones met Frank Dyer, the 1915 Pennsylvania State

champion. Dyer started fast against "the Kid from Dixie," winning five of the first six holes. Then Jones rallied. And what a rally. He played the next twenty-eight holes in a fraction over even 4s. It was the finest stretch of golf of the tournament. Jones won 4 and 2.

The victory vaulted Jones into the quarter-finals against Robert Gardner, the defending champion and winner of the 1909 U.S. Amateur and 1914 Chicago Open. Jones lost to Gardner 5 and 3. Gardner reached the finals only to be beaten by Chick Evans, the current U.S. Open champion (thus Evans became the first man to win the U.S. Open and Amateur championships in one year).

Still, in less than one week Bobby Jones had become famous, more famous than he ever imagined he would be. Never again would he enter a tournament unheralded. He became the outstanding youngster in the world of golf. Everyone who saw him at Merion in 1916 agreed that in a year or two his life would be glittering with golden victories. Although still a boy, he played like a man; and while it seemed to take such a long time for the boy to become a man, and even longer for him to become the giant of golf, that was only because Jones was in the national spotlight from the age of fourteen.

4

On September 22, 1930, the temperature and the humidity continued to climb in the eighties around the Philadelphia area. It was more like midsummer than fall. At the Merion Cricket Club, 7,000 spectators came out to watch the first of two qualifying rounds. As usual, Jones got the bulk of the gallery; he also got a guard force, a phalanx of fifty marines. Jones didn't disappoint his subjects, shooting a one-under-par 69 to lead the 169 qualifiers.

He had begun his round at 9:18 and finished exactly three hours later. This was his average time for a championship round of golf. Deep in concentration, he seriously began to study an approach shot as much as fifty yards before he reached his ball, so that when he did, he simply gave the shot one fast and final look, took his club, addressed the ball, and swung. There was no practice swing or prolonged study of the shot. After he hit the ball, he walked quickly, impatient to get on with the next shot.

The next day, Jones shot a 73, for a total of 142, which equaled the lowest qualifying score in a U.S. Amateur and qualified him as medalist. It was the sixth time Jones was either medalist or co-medalist in the Amateur, another unequaled record.

But Jones was furious coming off the last green. He had wanted to set the medalist record, but it had been an exceptionally slow round, having taken him just over three and a half hours.

At every tee that day at Merion, Jones had to wait. At the seventeenth tee he had to wait ten minutes. "Under these conditions," Jones later told reporters in one of his rare moments of public criticism, "it's like hitting your first drive eighteen times."

On the eighteenth tee, Jones took out his aggression on the ball. It flew off the clubhead of his driver, Jeanie Deans, and climbed and climbed, looking as if it would never come down. Finally, it landed near the bottom slope in the middle of the fairway and rolled through the small valley and up another slope. It ended up 345 yards from the tee, more than one-fifth of a mile. Never having been out so far, Jones misjudged his second shot. The ball landed on the rear of the green and rolled off. Jones's chip was weak, and he missed the putt for his par and the medalist record.

While Jones almost always proved otherwise, there is more to every tournament than the man who wins it. The 1930 U.S. Amateur was no exception. It was really two tournaments in one. There was the championship Jones was playing in, and then the championship in which the other thirty-one contestants were playing. From the point of view of exciting matches —where on every shot, on every long putt holed, the advantage can tip to one player to seize the match—the championship the thirty-one players were in was better.

Maurice McCarthy, Jr., a twenty-three-year-old Irishman with thick black hair and blue eyes, set a record that still stands of playing fifty holes of championship golf in one day. It began during the final qualifying round. He stood on the tee of the long par-3 seventeenth needing to birdie the final two holes, or play them in any total of only five shots, to make a play-off position. Using a driving iron, he hit directly at the pin on the seventeenth. The ball landed on the front of the green, rolled and rolled, hit the pin, and dropped softly into the cup, a hole-in-one. He played the eighteenth in four shots.

Early the next morning, with dew still on the ground, McCarthy had to play three extra holes, finally winning the third to become the thirty-second contestant in the 1930 Amateur. Then he faced his first opponent—Watts Gunn of Atlanta, once considered Jones's protégé. Back and forth the match went. On the eighteenth, McCarthy holed a long putt to square the match, and then won the first hole of the play-off.

He went to lunch for a welcome rest, well needed in light of who his afternoon opponent was to be. George Von Elm was the winner of the 1926 U.S. Amateur, a three-time member of the Walker Cup team, and the last player to beat Jones over thirty-six holes. He was twenty-eight, a man of direct German descent, of medium height, blond hair, blue eyes; he walked with a rather military bearing. After years of watching him play, O. B. Keeler wrote, "When the handsome Uhlan went swaggering down the fairway, you almost could hear the sabers clink."

McCarthy wasn't to be easily intimidated. After eighteen holes, in which the lead changed three times, the match was even; so for the fifth time that day, McCarthy played Merion's first hole. He parred it, as did Von Elm. They both birdied the second. From then on, they matched each other shot for shot. At the end of twenty-seven holes, the match still was even. At the short par-4 tenth, they both hit excellent drives. Von Elm pitched ten feet right of the pin. McCarthy played his favorite shot, a pitch and run. The ball rolled halfway across the green and finally came to rest less than three feet from the pin. An unnerved Von Elm missed his putt. McCarthy holed his. He had silenced the sabers.

On the same day, Jones had played just about half the number of holes as McCarthy, and sometimes not all that well: he kept dipping into patches of less than mediocre golf. It was the same old pattern of Jones playing badly when the going was good. But there was something else, something very rare in even the greatest of golfers. The best of Jones's game responded whenever he called on it.

On the way out of the locker room to play his first opponent, Jones met his friend Jess Sweetser coming in.

"Mornin', Sweets. Who're you going against this morning?"

"Philips Finlay," answered Sweetser.

"Good luck. He's a fine golfer."

"Who have you got this morning, Bob?"

"Sandy Somerville."

"Phew!" said Sweetser, "what a guy to get in the first round."

"I know."

It was actually a lucky thing that Jones's first opponent was a golfer for whom he had an earnest respect; it prevented Jones from becoming too complacent. Though Somerville wasn't all that well known in the United States, in his home country of Canada he was considered one of the best athletes. From 1922 to 1925 he had played varsity halfback on the University of Toronto football team, and center on the hockey team. He was good enough at hockey to turn professional. By 1930 he had won the Canadian Amateur golf championship three times. He would win it a total of five times, be runner-up three times, and in 1932 he would win the U.S. Amateur.

Sandy Somerville had a reputation for playing well under pressure, and against Jones he proved it. Through the first six holes, Somerville was even par; Jones was 1 under and 1 up. On the short par-4 seventh, they both pitched less than ten feet from the pin. Jones was away. It was a key putt. Jones wrote of it, "There is a chance right here for this match to swing one way or the other. On every hole it has been just a question of who would make a putt. I've got the first go at it this time. If I can get my ball into the hole, Sandy's putt will become a lot tougher; and if he should miss, it might mean the match. If I miss first, almost certainly he will hole and we will be even. If that happens, with Sandy in the mood he is today, I will be playing for my life from here in."

Jones carefully studied the slight right-to-left sidehill putt, all the time taking deep tranquilizing breaths. Using his small toylike putter, Calamity Jane, he gave the ball a light tap. The ball raced across the fast green, hesitated on the upper edge of the cup, and dropped. Somerville played the same line, but a shade too strong. Jones was 2 up. As he had anticipated, the seventh proved a pivotal hole. On the next one, Jones holed another good putt for a birdie, and on the ninth a 25-foot putt for another birdie. Jones was 4 up. He had played the outgoing nine in 32, four under par. Somerville was even par. Jones won 5 and 4.

At lunch Jones had only a chicken sandwich on toast and iced tea, as would be his noon ritual for the week. Once Jones had begun winning championships, he had given up his large lunches—no more feasts of ice cream. In fact, between rounds, his lunch often consisted of no more than tea and toast, and there had been times when his delicate stomach couldn't even keep that down. He thought he played his best golf fasting. Jones's counterpart on the tennis court, Bill Tilden, was quite the opposite. It wasn't unusual for Big Bill to devour a steak or two, a plate of home-fries, and a pot of steaming-hot coffee with plenty of sugar just half an hour before a big tennis match.

Having defeated Somerville, Jones faced his afternoon opponent—another Canadian, Fred Hoblitzel. As hot as Jones had been that morning, he suddenly cooled. He played the outgoing nine in ten strokes more, a sloppy 42. He was now playing just well enough to win. Hoblitzel had neither the game nor the nerves of Somerville, and his game cracked. Jones won, and though the margin of victory should have been more, it was, ironically, exactly as it had been that morning, 5 and 4.

The next day, Jones won his quarter-finals—the first of the thirty-six-hole matches—against Fay Coleman, the 1928 and 1930 Southern California champion. It was an uninspiring match with Jones winning 6 and 5.

All the matches that day were unspectacular. Emotionally and physically spent, a brave McCarthy lost to Sweetser 5 and 4.

On Friday, September 26, it would be Jones and Sweetser in the semi-finals. The other match would be between two lesser-known golfers, something of an East versus West match. Out of the West was a handsome blond, an eighteen-year-old by the name of Charlie Seaver. A muscular youth, he stood six feet tall and weighed 200 pounds; he looked more like a football player than a golfer. (He was both, and in a week he would be at Stanford University practicing for the varsity football team under "Pop" Warner.) Seaver had improved steadily every day of the championship, and some of the press were beginning to call him "the next Bobby Jones." Out of the East was Eugene Homans, a tall, lean young man of twenty-two from Englewood, New Jersey. He was a quiet, timid player, a religious Presbyterian who looked like he might be more at home behind the pulpit than on the golf course. He had learned to play golf at the age of ten from the 1924 U.S. Open champion, Cyril Walker.

Homans's golf swing was rather upright, loose, and wristy. He compensated for his lack of length off the tee with an excellent short game. And he was nothing if not tenacious. Five holes down to the young Californian after the first eighteen holes, Homans slowly whittled away at Seaver's lead. With two holes to play, he was only 1 down. He won the seventeenth to square the match, and when Seaver badly hooked his drive into the woods on the eighteenth, that was it. Homans won 1 up.

Seaver had come within one hole of making it to the finals of the U.S. Amateur. Ironically, as the years followed, neither Seaver nor Homans ever got past the third round of the U.S. Amateur. Today, Charlie Seaver is best known as the father of three-time Cy Young award winner, Tom Seaver.

Against his friend Sweetser, Jones got off to a fast start; he won four of the first five holes, which lulled him into a state of complacency. He proceeded to lose hole after hole. By the fourteenth hole, he held a precious 2-up lead. He won a hole back, and then Sweetser missed a 4-foot putt on the seventeenth green for a halve. Jones won the eighteenth, and went off to another lunch of chicken sandwich on toast and iced tea, 4 up.

Over the first six holes of the afternoon round, Jones only won two holes and halved the others. Then, from the seventh through the ninth holes, Jones went birdie, par, birdie—3, 4, 2—winning all three holes and was dormied going into the tenth hole.

After two good drives, Sweetser hit first, a high pitch to the right side of the tenth green. Then Jones hit a high mashie-niblick shot. The ball came down softly on the green, took a small bounce, and rolled to within ten inches of the pin. That was the match. Jones had won 10 and 8.

"Sweets," Jones said, as they walked to the clubhouse, "I feel sort of mean about that last shot. It was like a stab in the back, or a shot in the dark."

"Bob, it wasn't any shot in the dark. It was a great shot." And then he said, summing it up for all the players who had fallen all week before Jones, "I'd about had enough anyway."

The next day, Saturday, September 27, would be the most important day golf had ever known, that any sport has ever known.

The day broke cool and overcast. A blustery west wind had lowered the temperature and humidity by at least twenty degrees. The air was fresh, with a residue of rain from a thunderstorm that had come the previous evening. Suddenly, summer was gone and fall had arrived. It was the kind of day that helped turn the leaves on the oak, chestnut, and elm trees from green to yellow, amber and orange. In Pennsylvania, it was harvesttime.

The sun rose that morning at 5:48, hidden by clouds. Bobby Jones was up more than a half hour before. All week he had had trouble sleeping. Before going to bed, he would take a shot or two of corn whiskey, and with that plus fatigue he would quickly fall to sleep, only to wake around midnight.

Not since the 1926 British Amateur, played at Muirfield, The Honourable Company of Edinburgh Golfers, in which he had lost in the third round, had Jones been so troubled. Then he had spent the late evening hours in the fading glow of those long Scottish twilights, sitting by his hotel window watching Aberdeen Angus graze on a distant pasture.

Jones spent the dawn prowling anxiously around his hotel suite at the Barclay Hotel, smoking cigarette after cigarette. If his tee-off time had been 7:00 A.M., Jones would have been ready. But 9:15, the official tee-off time, was a long way off.

Jones dressed in a pair of light gray linen knickers, dark gray socks, a white cotton long-sleeved shirt, and a dark blue sleeveless sweater. When he got to the club, he changed into the same shoes he had worn all week, his favorite pair of handmade brown-and-white shoes.

By 8:30 a wall of spectators was beginning to line the fairways—four, five, and six deep, over 9,000 people. And they kept coming. Either they took the Paoli local, a train that travels up and down Philadelphia's Main Line, or they came by car and paid fifty cents for parking. By 10:00 A.M. all the parking spaces on the corner of Ardmore Avenue and Haverford Road, Turnbridge Road, College Avenue, and in the Wilson tract were filled.

Jones looked confident as well he should. His slimmest margin of victory had been 5 and 4. It had been four years, in the finals of the 1926 U.S. Amateur, since he had last been beaten over thirty-six holes. But inside, Jones's nerves were as tight as piano wire, and once again he was feeling slightly nauseous.

From the beginning, it was evident that Homans was struggling desperately with his nerves, and losing. He was painfully aware that he stood as the last obstacle between Jones and the

Grand Slam. No golfer ever has been in such a tormenting position.

Homans's swing tightened. Never long off the tee, he was shorter than usual, even though he was using a steel-shafted driver. Jones, using a spoon off the tee, was up to him. In the gusty winds, Homans continually misjudged his approaches to the green. It took him six holes before he got his first par.

In light of his opponent's misfortune, Jones could have run with the advantage, but he really wasn't winning any holes; rather, Homans was losing them. And the difference between the two can quickly catch up with a golfer. Jones had won only three holes while taking two bogeys. He bogeyed the seventh, a hole he had played beautifully all week. Homans parred it, and trimmed Jones's lead to 2 up. Wind or no wind, Jones seemed to be playing in some state of agony. Nothing seemed to be going very right, either. It wasn't anything he could really pinpoint.

Mickey Cochrane, the great catcher for the American League champions, the Philadelphia Athletics, was watching the match with an anxious O. B. Keeler. After seeing Jones miss several shots, which he could have made easily any other day, Cochrane told Keeler, "I know just how he feels. He is going after his fourth championship of the season, and it is just like a baseball club trying to win its fourth consecutive world's championship. He feels fine, but inwardly his nerves are seething, and when he gets ready to make a shot, he cannot get the proper grip. It's the old championship strain bearing down, and every ball player knows what that means."

Now suddenly with Homans pushing, Jones did what he had done all week—in fact, what he had done for the last five months. He accelerated his game. This was Jones, this was the

Jones the gallery, now numbering 12,000, had come to see. He played the remaining eleven holes in four 3s and seven 4s, an incoming nine of 33. He was invincible. Homans couldn't hold on against the incoming tide. At the end of the first eighteen holes, Jones was 7 up. He had scored a 72 to Homans's 79.

The gallery had expanded to a voluminous 18,000. It was no longer a question of whether Jones was going to win, but by how much. The gallery became almost hysterical, whooping and yelling every time Jones sank even the easiest putt.

So partisan was the gallery that one dispatcher, who all morning long had carefully noted each shot played, then raced back and forth to the pressroom with the results, was even denied lunch for not being faithful enough to Jones. It happened after he was relieved of his duties for the afternoon. The man sat on the back porch of the Merion clubhouse and ordered a small lunch for $1.50. Unfortunately, it was a course luncheon beginning with soup. As the man was about to dip his spoon into the soup, the headwaiter, who happened to have been Jones's personal waiter for the tournament, tapped him on the shoulder and officiously said, "You cannot eat your soup now. Mr. Jones is about to putt."

"But," the man said, "he's on the fourth green. He cannot hear me from this place with the high wind blowing against me."

"Nevertheless," said the waiter, "you must not eat your soup while Mr. Jones is addressing the ball in preparation for putting. That's final. If you persist I must remove your soup." So it went.

By the afternoon, the wind had lessened somewhat, and except for a few cumulus clouds, it was a brilliant, sunny afternoon. Jones and Homans and their caddies were flanked by marines, in addition to being surrounded by a cordon of

Jones's Atlanta friends. State troopers helped to marshal the frantic crowd.

For a few holes in the afternoon it looked as though Jones was continuing his magnificent play of the morning. On the third hole, he overshot the green, and his ball landed in the rear bunker. He took his concave wedge and just missed holing the explosion shot by two inches. He won the hole, and the next. He was 9 up.

Then, without any apparent warning, Jones suddenly yielded to the wave of tiredness of the week's play. His drives were not as long or as accurate. If he wasn't bunkered, he was in the rough. Putts didn't drop. He halved the next four holes, playing them in one over par. Jones lost the ninth. As the match dragged on, it began to seem like a popular play with one act too many. On the tenth hole, where the day before Jones had pitched to within ten inches of the pin, he hit his second shot into the left-side bunker guarding the green. Homans's shot followed Jones's. Homans was first to play; he skulled the ball and watched it skid across the green and roll into the bunker across the green. Jones stepped confidently into the bunker, quickly studied his shot, and swung. The ball popped up, followed by a cloud of fine white sand, hit the top lip of the bunker, and rolled back. Eighteen thousand people moaned. Both players took three more shots to finish the hole. It was only Jones's third double bogey in 151 holes of golf, but the match was beginning to look like a comedy of errors.

Going into the eleventh hole, Jones was dormied. He had only to tie or win one more hole, just one more hole, to win the Grand Slam. He looked tired and drawn, a man on the verge of emotional bankruptcy.

Merion's eleventh is short, just 378 yards. The tee shot is blind. One hundred yards from the tee the fairway drops abruptly into a narrow valley, with bunkers along the left side. The second shot is a pitch, or a short-iron shot to a small green shaped like Diana's helmet, set back and shaded by large oak, beech, and gum trees. A stream called the Baffling Brook flows fiendishly in front of the green, and around its right side and most of the rear. A shot too short will catch the stream, a shot slightly pushed will catch it, and a shot too long will catch it. Few golf holes engage the player with such foreboding.

It was by utter coincidence—a missed putt here, a flubbed bunker shot there—that Merion's eleventh gained its first historic passage into time. Eighteen thousand pairs of eyes gazed upon the cynosure in the sun, a man dressed in light gray linen knickers and a white cotton shirt. With his deceptively powerful swing, Bobby Jones sent the ball rocketing higher and higher into the sky. It seemed to stay in the air forever. Finally, the ball landed right in the middle of the fairway. The players moved down the fairway inside the sliding human knot. The gallery, sensing they were witnessing the end of a monumental trial in sports, swarmed about, jockeying for position, craning their necks to get a better view.

Homans, his expression as helpless as that of an outfielder chasing a home-run ball, hit first. It was a fine shot that finished eighteen feet above the pin. Jones looked quickly at the green. By now it was surrounded by thousands of people, standing on the banks of the stream. It seemed to him that he was hitting into a giant catcher's mitt.

He hit a high pitch shot; the ball easily cleared the Baffling Brook and dropped softly onto the green twenty feet below the pin. A giant roar echoed throughout the valley.

Jones stood over his putt and studied the line quickly. It was so quiet you could have heard a pin drop on the grass.

Jones gave the ball a firm tap. The ball rolled up the slight incline, broke a foot left and stopped ten inches from the cup. Homans wasted little time with his putt. It wasn't the easiest putt, and under the circumstances any putt he had to make to stay in the match was an incredibly difficult putt. He gave it a brave try. The ball trickled down the slope, but before it even got halfway to the cup, it swerved right. It wouldn't be. He immediately conceded Jones his putt and walked to shake his hand.

For a moment there was silence. Then it began—the shrieks, the howls, the applause, a roar building to a mighty crescendo. There was a stampede toward the green, but the marines were there first and drew their protective knot around Jones, Homans, and their caddies. Finally, a corridor was formed, packed thickly with people up the twelfth hole, across Ardmore Avenue, and to the clubhouse.

The cheers continued. They were not just for the 1930 U.S. Amateur. The cheers were also for the British Amateur at St. Andrews, where several times victory seemed to hang by the thinnest thread; for the British Open at Hoylake, where Jones just carried on and on until at the very last stretch he pulled his game together, and then waited, experiencing the internal shrilling of the nerves as other players fell away; and for the U.S. Open at Interlachen, where he had risen to his greatest powers. While the cheers were for Jones, the new Amateur champion, they weren't so much for this championship's matches, which had lacked the drama of the other championships, as they were for the fact that the final trick had been pulled off, the final line drawn. No longer would there be an "impregnable quadrilateral." Jones had given a sense of certainty to the most uncertain of games. Momentarily, he had mended a flawed world. In Jones's possession were the gold and silver trophies and medals of the British Amateur and Open and the United States Amateur and Open championships: the Grand Slam. In the future, golfers would follow as best they could.

The walk to the clubhouse seemed to take forever. Of that walk, William Richardson of *The New York Times* wrote, "It was the most triumphant journey that any man ever travelled in sport." Tired, worry-worn, and looking older, so much older than twenty-eight, Jones acknowledged as best he could the cheers of his subjects, quite unable to digest the fact that the almost superhuman task he had set for himself was over at last. It seemed such a long time ago when it all had begun, though it was really only May of that year.

In total, Jones had actually played only twenty days of championship golf over four months; but on half those days, he had been scheduled to play thirty-six holes. He had played 475 holes of golf. In the British and U.S. Opens, at stroke play, he had averaged 72.5 strokes. At Merion, Jones played 152 holes, in approximately seventeen strokes over par, or more precisely four over even fours.

All day Saturday, September 27, every phone in the sports department of the *Atlanta Journal* had been covered. Callers would only hear "Jones is 3 up," or "Jones is 6 up," and so on. After Jones won, Ernest Rogers, a senior reporter, phoned Mrs. Bobby Jones and told her of her husband's victory.

"That's grand," she said. "After the morning round I thought he would win, but it is a comfort to know it's all over."

Pandemonium ran through Merion's small clubhouse. Despite this being Prohibition, champagne, corn whiskey, and bathtub gin flowed as swiftly as the Baffling Brook. Big Bob, lost in the crowd, ran around wildly saying, "Where's my boy? Where's my boy?"

The Havermeyer Trophy, named after the first president of the USGA, and presented to the winner of the U.S. Amateur, sat in the middle of a table by the first tee. The table was covered with a spotless white linen tablecloth that sporadically flapped in the breeze.

After Jones accepted the trophy, he said in a speech shrouded with ambivalence, "I expect to continue to play golf, but just when and where I cannot say now. I have no definite plans either to retire or as to when and where I may continue in competition. I might play next year and lay off in 1932. I might stay out of the battle next season and feel like another tournament the following year. That's all I can say about it now."

The speech was characteristic of Jones for its conciseness, but uncharacteristic for its vagueness. In truth, it was a flat denial, for after he had won that year's U.S. Open Jones had vowed that if he won the U.S. Amateur, he would retire from competition.

At least so the press in the clubhouse at the Interlachen Country Club in Minneapolis had been told.

"What are you going to do when you retire?" one reporter had asked Jones after he won his fourth U.S. Open.

Jones took a sip of a highball of corn whiskey, and grinning with a mischievous gleam in his eyes, he turned to his Boswell, O. B. Keeler, also celebrating, and said, "You'd better tell them, O. B. You know."

Keeler, who had just come out of the shower, fastened a towel around his waist, and with a drink in hand climbed up on one of the benches to perform one of his favorite pastimes, reciting poetry. He could recite poetry for hours, but this time it was brief, and from Hilaire Belloc:

> If I ever become a rich man,
> Or if ever I grow to be old,
> I will build a house with a deep thatch
> To shelter me from the cold,
> I will hold my house in the high woods
> Within a walk of the sea,
> And the men that were boys when I was a boy
> Shall sit and drink with me.

PART TWO

The Journey Begins

5

A national golf championship isn't always fair, isn't always sensible, and is rarely any fun. By 1930 no golfer knew more about this than Bobby Jones. Already he had played for twenty-eight national titles; he had won nine, more than any other golfer. Sometimes he had made it look easy, but it never, never was. He had learned for that vital moment how to still his nerves—which otherwise would be jumping like jackhammers—so he could pull off the shot; and he always seemed to do it with the dignity and grace of a bishop.

In 1930 Jones had set up for himself an agonizing schedule, to play in three national golf championships in less than seven and a half weeks, and in a fourth two months later. The few people to whom Jones revealed his plans believed his march for the Grand Slam began early that year.

The truth was that the idea of winning all four national championships in a single year had been gnawing at Jones since 1926. That May he had lost the British Amateur for the second time. Feeling disgusted with himself, especially because he felt he had let down his British admirers, he stayed on in Great Britain to compete in the British Open. In dramatic fashion he won. Less than a month later, he captured the U.S. Open, making him the first golfer to hold both crowns in a single year.

At that moment Jones started to believe that if he could beat the professionals, there was a fair possibility he could beat the amateurs. Provided the circumstances were favorable, he thought he might be able to win both Amateurs and Opens in one year. In 1926 he looked ahead and logically concluded that 1930 was the best possible year. The Walker Cup matches were being played in England, and he could stay to play in the British Amateur and Open without having to make another transatlantic crossing.

In January 1930, Jones announced his plans to attempt to annex the four national championships. He initially told only three people: his wife, his father, and O. B. Keeler. Then every day after work that winter—a cold and drizzling one in Atlanta—Jones left his law offices on Cone Street and went to the deserted Atlanta Theatre. There he began preparing for his upcoming campaign in what has to be one of the strangest ways any great golfer ever prepared for any season.

Jones played a game called "Doug." Its proper name was Dougledyas, named after its inventor, Douglas Fairbanks, one of many movie stars who befriended Jones. As a gesture of their friendship, Fairbanks sent Jones a net, some paddles, and shuttlecocks. The game was a cross between tennis and badminton. Ten-minute volleys were common. It was a game of speed, placement of the shuttlecock, and constant running.

Jones played it more enthusiastically than well, essentially because he was a slow man on his feet. His huge thighs and thick legs, the base of a power that could propel a golf ball more than a fifth of a mile in the air, were not the legs of a runner. Jones's prime motivation for playing was to help keep his weight down. During the winter, he usually gained fifteen to twenty pounds—up to 190.

Never a man to take himself too seriously, Jones did have his vain spots, and number one was his waistline. Jokingly, O. B. Keeler wrote about Jones that winter, "He might be getting a bit vain about his waistline—that is, I should say, sensitive. He might be vain about it, if there were not so much of it."

Even so, Keeler was fearful Jones might pull a muscle or tear a tendon, and he tried to persuade him to stop playing "Doug." Keeler even went so far as to seek support from Harry Mehre, then the football coach of the University of Georgia. "I regard golfing championships as of more importance than waistlines," the coach said.

As far as Jones was concerned, playing "Doug" was just about enough for him, and he was very right. It kept his weight down, and his competitive spirit sharp, which was all he wanted. After all, to Jones golf was a game, not a business. To round out his training schedule, he decided to play in two warm-up tournaments late that spring of 1930 before the national championships. This was a lot of competitive golf for Jones, six tournaments in one year. Only once, when he was eighteen, had he played in more. He had played in eight and had won three of them. Since then, however, he had severely limited his tournament schedule. He played in tournaments only to sharpen his game for major championships. From 1921 to 1929, other than national championships and exhibitions, Jones played in only six regular tournaments. He won half of them. He so limited his schedule that in 1928 and 1929, including national championships, Jones played in only five events; he won three, including the U.S. Open and Amateur.

In early February 1930, Jones began playing golf several days a week. By Saturday, February 15, he had pretty much whipped his game into shape. That day, he toured East Lake in 63, nine under par.

Now he was ready for his initial tournament of the year: the first Savannah Open. Its total purse was $3,000, with $1,000 going to the low professional. It was being played over the Savannah Golf Club, one of the first golf clubs in the United States, initially founded in 1796. It was a short 6,206-yard course with a par of 72.

The tournament turned into a battle between Jones and his new friend Horton Smith, who then was only twenty-two but already the winner of nine tournaments, and the leading professional money winner. Jones opened with a 67 to break the course record. He played the front nine in 32, a score helped much with two birdie 3s at the second and fifth holes, which respectively measured 271 yards and 251 yards; Jones reached both greens in one with a spoon off the tee.

The next day, Jones played the same nine in 40, taking a seven on the second hole. Smith responded by breaking Jones's record, shooting a 66. Now he led Jones by five shots. The next day, with thirty-six holes scheduled, Jones caught Smith in the third round, shooting a brilliant round of 65, again setting a course record. He had nine 4s, five 3s, two 2s, and two 5s.

The final round was a gallant duel. Both men played the first six holes in one under par, and were all even. Then on the par-5 seventh, Jones bogeyed and Smith birdied. By the time Jones reached the sixteenth hole, he was only one stroke behind. Then he missed a 4-foot birdie putt. Knowing he needed to birdie the par-5 seventeenth, Jones went for the green in two and hooked a spoon shot out-of-bounds, taking a bogey 6. With a last desperate gasp, he rolled in a 30-foot putt for a birdie 3 on the eighteenth. But Smith finished smoothly with two 4s for a total of 278 and won by one stroke. He collected $1,000, boosting his fall and winter earnings to over $11,000.

As low amateur, Jones received a 12-gauge double-barreled shotgun. Jones had broken the course record twice, and finished nine under par. The Savannah Open would never be played again, and it was truly the last golf tournament Bobby Jones lost.

On March 31 and April 1, Jones, just having turned twenty-eight, played in the Southeastern Open in Augusta, Georgia. It was a seventy-two-hole event with thirty-six holes played each day over the Augusta Country Club and the Forrest-Hills Ricker course; both courses played to over 6,600 yards. The tournament was the last of the makeshift fall-winter tour. For years at the Masters, Jones would point toward the Augusta Country Club, which borders the Augusta National Golf Club, and tell friends, "That's where I played my finest golf of 1930."

The promoters of the Southeastern Open hoped for another fierce duel between Jones and Horton Smith. After the first thirty-six holes, Jones led by three shots, shooting rounds of even par. Smith was second. It still looked like a duel.

It had been a day not unlike many thereafter at the Masters, when the key to scoring depended on one's putting skills. The greens were hard and absolutely shone in the bright March sunlight. It was like putting on a sheet of wavy ice. One player confessed that when he walked on the greens he was fearful his feet would skid out from under him. Three-putting was common. Gene Sarazen four-putted one green. Jones three-putted only once.

The next day, Jones shot a morning round of 69; Smith clung to second place but slipped to a 76. Going into the final round, Jones had a ten-shot lead. He started his final round with three 3s—a birdie, an eagle, and a birdie—followed by six pars for a 32. By the time Jones reached the sixteenth, a par 3, he had taken only 54 strokes. All he had to do was finish with three pars for a course record of 66 and a win by eighteen shots.

At the sixteenth, a logjam had formed, forcing Jones to wait for four foursomes to play out. He spent the time talking to Grantland Rice and Ty Cobb. Time slipped by. A half hour passed. It was finally Jones's turn to play. He promptly hooked his tee shot into the woods, hit his next into the greenside bunker, and ended up three-putting for a triple bogey. He parred the next hole, and then double-bogeyed the eighteenth. He had again fallen into his familiar pattern of mental complacency.

Afterward, Cobb gave Jones the dressing-down of his life. To Cobb the idea of winning was not just to win, but to win by as much as possible.

Actually that was what Jones had done. His triumph over the pros was his most decisive victory. He had given them a thorough thrashing. He had beaten Horton Smith, who finished second and collected $1,000, by thirteen strokes; he had beaten Joe Turnesa by fifteen, Johnny Farrell by sixteen, Gene Sarazen by twenty-seven, and Bobby Cruickshank by twenty-nine strokes.

Cruickshank, who had finished just ahead of Jones, simply shook his head in amazement as he watched Jones toy with the field. He told O. B. Keeler, "Bob is just too good. He's going to win the British Amateur and British Open, and then he's coming back here and win the National Open and National Amateur. They'll never stop him this year."

It was a bold prophecy by an even bolder man. Cruickshank, a Scot, sent $500 to his father-in-law in Great Britain to place a bet with a bookmaker that Jones would win all four national championships that year. The bookmaker placed the odds realistically at 120 to 1. When Jones beat Eugene Homans on September 27, 1930, Cruickshank collected $60,000.

On May 4, 1930, Jones's quest for the Grand Slam began in earnest. With his wife, Mary, O. B. Keeler, and a flock of friends from Atlanta, he sailed for England aboard the *Mauretania*. Also on board were seven of the United States' best available golfers, who along with Jones represented the United States in the Walker Cup matches. Two of them, Harrison Johnston and George Voigt, literally came within inches of robbing Jones of the British Amateur championship.

In all, it was a festive crossing. The passenger list included Maurice Chevalier, the art dealer Sir Joseph Duveen, Harry Lauder, and Douglas Fairbanks. Fairbanks was going specifically to watch Jones in the Walker Cup matches, but because of pressing business in New York later that month, he couldn't stay longer to watch Jones in the British Amateur. He promised to return to watch him in the British Open.

6

There was no magical moment when Bobby Jones first gave the world a boyish smile, a nod of the head, or emoted a range of feelings, no instant forever frozen in time when he captured a world of worshipers. It began gradually.

At the Merion Cricket Club in the 1916 U.S. Amateur, fourteen-year-old Jones was the sensation of the tournament. He was the valiant underdog, aggressive on the course and painfully shy off it. There was also a certain aura of mystery about the youngster, being a Southerner playing a game so very well that was then strongly dominated by Northeasterners. But, of course, the initial attraction was his style, the way he played. With a swing of such exquisite grace and evenness it made the swings of other players appear bumpy and ragged, Jones spanked drives over 250 yards and hit his irons with decisive crispness.

Even "the Great Old Man," as Walter J. Travis was called,

was swept up in the praise of Jones. Now this was something. Although only fifty-four years old, Travis sported a beard as white as the sand of Merion's bunkers. In 1908 he had founded and edited the *American Golfer* magazine. No one, not even Bernard Darwin, could match Travis for breadth of knowledge of golf. The game was not just a way of life with Travis, it was life itself. He once wrote a 7,000-word essay on the Versailles Conference almost entirely in golf terms.

When Travis was asked about young Jones, he stroked his white beard and said, "Improvement? He can never improve on his shots, if that's what you mean. But he will learn a great deal more about playing them. And his putting method is faulty."

Old Walter Travis was right. Until 1922, when he got a putting lesson from Travis, Jones remained only an average putter. Then in one season he became one of the best putters in the game. For centuries, golfers believed in the putting theory that if you were never up to the hole with the ball, you were never in. Jones rejected this theory. "Of course," he once said, "we never know but that the ball which is on line and stops short would have holed out. But we do know that the ball that ran past did not hole out." Thereafter, Jones played all his putts to die at the hole.

It was learning how to play his shots, wisely using his power and keeping his thunderous temper in check, that took Jones so very long. The years went by, each seeming like a decade, as national championship after championship, eleven in all, eluded him. Sometimes Jones lost simply because he was out-played; other times he was unlucky, or lacked experience, or his temper got in his way. Unfortunately, it all added up to the same thing for Jones: he had failed, and with each defeat, a certain sheen of his polish of promise faded. Sure Jones was good, the sportswriters were writing, but he couldn't handle the pressure to win the big ones.

However, he did win a half dozen other important tournaments. His first important victory was in June 1917; Jones then was just fifteen years and three months old. He became the youngest player ever to win the Southern Amateur. Sixty-four of the finest amateurs in the South and Southwest gathered at the Roebuck Springs Country Club in Birmingham, Alabama. In the fourth round, Jones defeated Reuben Bush, the defending champion.

In the finals, Jones's opponent was Louis Jacoby, a man more than twice his age and a very deliberate player. At one point in the match, Jacoby studied a spoon shot so long that one of the thousands of spectators remarked, "What's he waiting for?"

"Oh," said another spectator, "he's waiting for the grass to grow up under his ball to give him a better lie."

At the end of the first eighteen holes of the thirty-six-hole finals, Jones was 4 up. At lunch, Jones had what was then his usual big meal, complete with apple pie served with two large scoops of ice cream. The added calories didn't help. Jones lost the first three holes. Now he was only 1 up. At the fourth, a long par 3, Jones rifled a mid-iron shot. The ball went straight for the pin, danced about the cup, and stopped three inches away. That was the match. From then on, Jones played near-flawless golf and beat Jacoby 6 and 4. The youngster was cool and almost machinelike as he clicked off pars and birdies. He was playing like a man, but when Jacoby congratulated the youngster, suddenly Jones's face flushed with embarrassment: he was the schoolboy again. The only thing he could think of saying was "Much obliged, Mr. Jacoby."

So by the time he was only fifteen, Bobby Jones had won the Georgia State Amateur, was a quarter-finalist in the U.S. Amateur, and had won the Southern Amateur. He knew he was a crackerjack golfer; the American golfing public would be his witness for the remainder of 1917 and 1918.

Now with the advent of United States involvement in World War I, the USGA and most sectional golf associations canceled their championships. Yet the war years were good for Jones, and he was good for the war effort. He did exactly what he loved to do—played golf with his old friends and made new ones. It didn't make too much difference that his golf was in the form of exhibitions in front of huge galleries, sometimes playing thirty-six holes a day. He simply was roaming the country having the time of his young life. When it was all over in 1918, he was quite astonished to learn that he had helped raise $150,000. It was difficult for him to comprehend it all. After all, he was just a kid having fun.

Most of the proceeds went to the Red Cross. In 1917 J. A. Scott of the Wright and Ditson Company—then a prominent sporting goods firm—started booking Red Cross matches starring Bobby Jones, his friend Perry Adair, their friend Alexa Stirling, who in 1916 had won the U.S. Women's Amateur, and Chicago's fine woman golfer, Elaine Rosenthal.

They played better-ball matches. One day Jones would be partnered with Stirling and Adair with Rosenthal; the next day the order would be changed. As Jones's reputation as a top player preceded him, so did his reputation for having an explosive temper. Sometimes, to horrified galleries, he threw his club after he missed a shot; if he missed an easy putt, he would pick up the ball, wind up in a pitcher's motion, and throw the ball into the woods.

After one such incident, Alexa Stirling, a gentle, even-

tempered woman, berated him about his unsportsmanlike behavior. Jones snapped back, "I don't give a damn what anybody thinks about me. I only get mad at myself." That was
the truth. In unkind moments, the sportswriters called Jones
"a hot-blooded Southerner" or "a sorehead."

Even so, the golfers were acclaimed as fine young patriots,
and Jones and Adair felt very snappy as they played their way
through the Northeast and Midwest wearing their Swiss
Guard caps. The Red Cross matches ended late in the summer
of 1917; the next year they were replaced by the War Relief
matches. Now Jones and Adair and other top amateurs were
pitted against the pros. It was Jones's first time taking on the
professionals in earnest.

In a warm-up match, Jones got his first taste of psychological warfare. He and Adair were playing two pros in a four-ball
match. Jones started off with two birdie 3s. "Well, Bobby,"
said one of the pros as they walked to the next tee, "you know
eighteen threes make fifty-four."

Jones began thinking about that. He never made another 3,
struggled to make 4s, and ended up with 80. It made for an
ominous beginning, but Jones was learning. All through that
summer, he, Adair, Chick Evans (the reigning U.S. Amateur
and Open champion), Robert Gardner (the 1909 and 1915
U.S. Amateur champion), Francis Ouimet (winner of the 1913
U.S. Open and the 1914 U.S. Amateur), Jerry Travers (four-
time winner of the U.S. Amateur), and Max Marston took on
the pros. In alternate-shot play, Jones was good but beaten
several times; however, in the singles matches against the pros,
Jones was the only amateur who wasn't defeated.

He was just sixteen at the time. That June he had graduated
near the top of his class at Tech High School in Atlanta and in
September, he entered Georgia Tech. Until the next spring, he

played very little golf. He didn't have time. Majoring in mechanical engineering, Jones's curriculum was English, mathematics, chemistry, physics, geology, and mechanical drawing. He pledged the fraternity Sigma Alpha Epsilon.

But in the wake of the scores of exhibitions Jones had played, he had left a golfing population inspired by his swing, annoyed at him for his temper, but most of all itching with curiosity to know more about him. How could he rifle a ball with a mid-iron 200 yards? How did he drive a golf ball 250 yards? Who was Stewart Maiden, from whom Jones had copied his swing and taken an occasional lesson, and who also taught Alexa Stirling and Perry Adair?

In 1919 Grantland Rice, then editor of the *American Golfer* magazine, set out to satisfy the curiosity of his readers. He hired O. B. Keeler as a contributing editor. Many golfers believed Keeler had the best possible jobs of all jobs. He was then reporting on Jones, Stirling, and Adair for the *Georgian*, and writing at more length about them for the magazine. But as sure as no job is without its occasional thorns that prick one's patience and fortitude, neither was Keeler's. Keeler had a very sharp thorn in his side: the most famous golf instructor of the time, Stewart Maiden. A conversation of more than three sentences from Maiden about the golf swing and the theory of the swing was long. One instruction piece for the *American Golfer* on the most common fault in golf verged on the comic-surreal.

"Well, I'm ready," announced Keeler with pad and pencil in hand.

"Good. Where are you going?" replied Maiden.

"Nowhere until I find out about the commonest fault of golfers. . . . A fault always hinges on something. What does the commonest fault in golf turn on?"

"I suppose you'd say it turns on the pivot," answered Maiden.

"What if you don't pivot?" asked Keeler.

"Then you don't shoot golf. Everyone pivots—everyone that shoots golf. There is no other way."

"But some golfers pivot more than others, don't they?"

"I don't think so."

"Doesn't a flat swinger pivot more than an upright swinger?"

"Not so you notice it," answered Maiden. "I keep telling you that all good golfers hit the ball practically the same way. And they all pivot."

"Well," said Keeler, losing his patience, "that brings us back to the start of the backswing. How do you start the thing, anyway?"

"The way that gets the best results for the player. I tell my pupils to start everything at once, hands, club, hips, and shoulders."

"That is," Keeler asked, "push with the left and pull with the right?"

"There you go again! There's too much stuff written and taught about 'left' and 'right' and about all it does is mix up the player. . . . Take the club back with an easy pivot and don't bother about it. When the club is back, bring it down the same way."

"I've heard," said Keeler, "some good players say they start the downward swing with the left hip."

"Maybe they do," answered Maiden. "I never watched with a microscope."

"Then, you are not conscious of 'throwing down' the club with the right hand or 'starting' it with the left?"

"I'm not conscious of any part of the swing after I start the club back," replied Maiden, "and I don't believe anybody else is, no matter how much they talk about it."

"You don't mean to say you hit the ball with a blank mind?"

"Yes, I do."

"But," asked an exasperated Keeler, "if you're playing different kinds of shots—the push shot, the pitch-and-run, the intentional slice?"

"Do your thinking before you start the swing. You won't be likely to do it afterward. That's a common fault too, trying to think after the stroke is started."

Keeler tried one more approach to get a definite answer from Maiden. "So you think," Keeler asked, "that trying to pivot in sections, or failing to pivot enough, is the commonest fault?"

"I didn't say so," replied Maiden.

Keeler was proof that an intelligent man with reasonable coordination could spend half his adult life around the best golfers and teachers, and never be anything better than an average golfer, a regular 90-shooter.

His appearance was deceptive. A big compact man of just over six feet with broad, rounded shoulders and a short thick torso, Keeler looked like a man who could knock the cover off a golf ball, drive it the length of Peachtree Street. He never came close. And just when he discovered another of golf's hidden secrets, in his early forties, he was stricken with severe rheumatism. After several operations, he was left with a stiffened, slightly but permanently bent left knee. When he walked, he resembled a place-kicker just about to step into the kick. Despite his physical handicap, and for all his theorizing, rationalizing, and analyzing about golf, it was a wonder he could hit the ball at all, even for his most common shot: the slice.

About the mystery of golf, Keeler liked to be compared with the wise philosophers. He wrote, "Golf is a game of infinite exigency; and its divergencies are not sharply lined, but diffused." Of the missed in golf, he wrote, "The terrible thing about a missed shot in golf is that the thing is done, irrevocably, irretrievably. Perhaps that is why golf is so great a game; it is so much like the game of life. We don't have the shots over in either."

Keeler knew about the missed shots of life, and would have just as soon forgotten them, for until Jones came along, he was just another good reporter, and felt he had been lucky enough to get that far. Of all the great sportswriters of the Golden Age of Sport—Grantland Rice, Westbrook Pegler, Ring Lardner, W. O. McGeehan, Bud Kelland, Paul Gallico, Al Laney, Damon Runyon, Dan Parker, John Kieran, Ralph McGill, and Alan Gould—undoubtedly Keeler was the luckiest. He was the right man, at the right time, in the right place.

Oscar Bane Keeler was born on June 4, 1882, the oldest son of a successful businessman who in 1886 moved his family from Chicago to Nelson, Georgia, and became superintendent of a marble quarry. Four years later he retired to Marietta, Georgia, where O. B. graduated from high school, having distinguished himself as a first-rate student, taking four years of Latin and Greek and becoming a voracious reader who remembered just about everything he read.

Then for ten sad years, Keeler drifted from job to job. He had yet to find himself, and to add to his burden he was married and the father of two children. If anything kept up his spirits, it was that he was an easy laugher and could even see humor in the dark side of life.

At 7:30 Monday morning, January 4, 1909, Keeler arrived for work at the *Georgian* as a reporter. Except for a few verses on sport, he had never had anything published. Under the terms of the agreement with the city editor, Keeler was to work for a two-week trial period without pay and supply his own typewriter.

Keeler was sent out on a routine assignment to cover the regular Monday morning meeting of the Baptist Minister's Alliance. The key address that morning was delivered by Dr. Len Boughton, then the flaming firebrand of Dixie ministry. His topic was psychic healing of physical illness.

Keeler realized the sensational news value of the address at such a placid time in America. When he returned to the paper he asked the city editor how much he should write. The reply was appropriately terse and wise. "Keeler," the editor said, "write as much as you can make interesting."

The new reporter did, and the story made page one. Before Keeler's trial weeks were up, he was on the payroll and then switched to the sports department. A year later he joined the *Kansas City Star,* and then in 1913 returned to the *Georgian,* just in time to cover Jones's first appearance in the Southern Amateur. Finally, after years of coaxing by Major John Cohen, Keeler joined the *Atlanta Journal.* His major assignment with an expense-be-damned policy was to cover Bobby Jones.

In all of sport, no athlete ever had a more faithful reporter than Jones had in Keeler. They were together in the thirty-one national championships Jones played in, plus scores of other tournaments. Keeler was one of only two American reporters at the 1930 British Amateur and Open. (The other being Al

Laney from the Paris bureau of the *Herald Tribune*.) In all, by train, boat, and car, Keeler traveled more than 120,000 miles with Jones. Keeler also covered eight national championships in which Alexa Stirling played.

As the sole chronicler of Bobby Jones, Keeler was vaulted into national prominence and ranked as one of the top sportswriters. He knew more about Jones than anyone else, including his family. And while he was biased toward his favorite subject, he was not above taking an occasional rhetorical poke at Jones. More than once Jones said, "O. B., I didn't play very good today." Keeler quoted Jones exactly, then added, "That's what Bobby told me this afternoon, ungrammatically."

When Jones lost, Keeler didn't find it hard to praise the play of an opponent—which, of course, had to be good if the man beat Jones. The loyalty between the two men was unique, all the more so as athletes then were beginning to distrust sportswriters, who were just beginning to write more truthfully about them. The great columnist W. O. McGeehan of the *Herald Tribune*, who was a good friend of the heavyweight fighter Gene Tunney, but disliked Tunney's intellectual pretense, destroyed their friendship with one sentence after Tunney wrote a book about his fighting experiences. McGeehan's review: "Gene Tunney has written one book after reading several others . . ."

Nothing like that could have happened between Jones and Keeler. Keeler never betrayed Jones; and while Jones was perhaps singularly responsible for promoting Keeler's career, when the final putt was holed, it's hard to say who did more for whom.

While Maiden handled the mechanics of Jones's swing, Keeler handled the mental side. When Jones's father, "The

Colonel," as he was beginning to be called in the early 1920s, stopped accompanying his son to national championships because he felt his presence was jinxing the boy, Keeler became the surrogate father. Every time just before Jones and Keeler boarded a train, Clara Jones would take Keeler aside and say, "O. B., you look after Robert now." Keeler was other things as well—Jones's friend, the older brother he never had, and coach.

Before Jones started to win, it was Keeler—ever the golfing analyst—who realized that Bobby was losing strokes on the putting greens in afternoon matches. Jones was beginning to call it fate.

"Fate, hell," Keeler replied after Jones was beaten one afternoon. "You eat like a ditch digger at noon and then wonder why you don't quite have that extra 'feel' in the afternoon. Many a hearty lunch has cost thousands of golfers a good round later on. The nerve center of the body and the digestive center are only an inch or so apart. They can't both work well at the same time." Thus, from 1922 on, Jones's lunch usually consisted of a light toasted sandwich and tea.

At no time was Keeler more valuable to Jones than from 1916 to 1922, when Jones failed to win a national championship. Keeler, who himself knew about the frustration of hard times, called these Jones's "seven lean years."

He called 1919 Jones's "Runner-up Year." Jones played in four tournaments—two sectional titles, and two national championships. He finished second in three of them, and lost in the semi-finals of the other. In each tournament of that year seventeen-year-old Jones gained some kernel of knowledge.

Ironically, much later in life, Jones said, "I never learned anything from a tournament I won. . . ."

The first event was the Southern Amateur, played at the

New Orleans Country Club. Both Jones and Keeler believed it was being played at the most diabolical of times, a week before the scheduled establishment of national prohibition. Jones lost in the semi-finals 6 and 5.

On the very first shot of the tournament, Jones hit a mashie shot of 150 yards. The ball was badly pulled, so much so it even missed the bunker left of the green, and ended up in a wheelbarrow, lodged on an old rusty horseshoe. Keeler saw the humor of the whole situation and was just about doubled over with laughter. Jones was furious, and damned if he was going to take a penalty stroke. He didn't know he was entitled to a free drop, the wheelbarrow being "an unnatural hazard." Jones studied the shot carefully. His only hope was to go after the horseshoe. He took his niblick and walloped the horseshoe. Out it flew and onto the green. The ball trickled free. Jones got his four and lost only one stroke to par, but from then on, Jones studied the rules of golf as carefully as he would later study law books.

The 1919 U.S. Amateur was played at the Oakmont Country Club outside of Pittsburgh. Jones advanced easily to the finals where he met Davidson Herron, a member of the club, and who, at age twenty, was the second youngest player in the field after Jones.

The match was even after the first eighteen holes of the thirty-six-hole finals. Then Herron, who knew the treacherous slick greens of Oakmont, made several long putts. At the twelfth hole, a 621-yard par 5, he was 3 up, but his prospects for holding the lead were slim. His drive caught a fairway bunker, and his recovery was weak. Jones's drive was straight down the middle. Now Jones had the advantage: he was going for the green in two with a brassie. But just as he reached the top of his backswing, a marshal with a megaphone yelled to clear the gallery by the green. With the sudden burst of noise, Jones flinched, and half-topped his shot. He was fuming, wild with anger. He lost the match 5 and 4.

Jones's choleric nature then could be triggered by some of the most seemingly insignificant incidents. In the 1920 U.S. Amateur, Jones met Francis Ouimet in the semi-finals. Ouimet was playing very well, and surely would have won the match anyway, but Jones made it easier for him. On the seventh green, the twenty-fifth hole of the match, Jones was studying a long putt when a bee landed on his ball. Jones boiled. To a horrified and snickering gallery, Jones, waving his putter madly like a battle sword, chased the bee across the green. He then three-putted. Ouimet won 6 and 5. The worst was still to come.

In 1921 Jones made his first trip to Great Britain. The British called him "Bonnie Bobby." The "Bonnie" was quickly dropped, but the Bobby stayed, and the youth, who until then had been known by his full name of Robert T. Jones, Jr., would forever be known simply as Bobby Jones.

He was so handsome. His wheat-colored hair was parted down the left side of the large head, and he dressed rather conservatively in fawn-colored knickers, handmade shoes always highly polished, and cashmere sweaters. His shyness, modesty, and feeling for the understated were qualities the British loved. If there ever was for them a prince of golf, "Bonnie Bobby" Jones was it. He was cheered everywhere he went. Although he lost in the fourth round of the British Amateur, the British knew he would win it someday. And if one of their own wasn't going to win The Open (as the British Open always is referred to in Great Britain), they hoped Jones would.

The championship was being played over the Old Course at St. Andrews. Not unlike so many Americans who first play the

7. Jones at St. Andrews, Scotland, during the
first round of the 1930 British Amateur, the
first of the four national championships of the
Grand Slam. On the fourth hole, his drive
landed in a bunker called the "Cottage," 140
yards from the green. From there Jones holed
out for an eagle 2. He won 3 and 2.

8. Triumphantly, Jones walks off the eighteenth green after beating George Voigt in
the semi-finals of the British Amateur. The
two friends had a fierce duel. After thirteen
holes, Jones was 2 down with five holes to
play. He beat Voigt 1 up, Jones's third victory
in the championship by the slimmest of
margins.

9. In the thirty-six-hole finals, Jones faced the Englishman Roger Wethered (in the foreground), winner of the 1923 British Amateur. Here they walk toward the seventeenth tee. Jones is 5 up.

10. On the eighteenth green, Jones putts for a birdie as Wethered watches. In the background is the famed clubhouse of the Royal and Ancient. The hollow in the left front of the green is called the "Valley of Sin." Jones eventually beat Wethered 7 and 6.

11. Jones driving during the second round of the 1930 British Open at the Royal Liverpool Golf Club, Hoylake, England. He played his sloppiest golf of the year during this championship.

12. Jones blasts out of a bunker on the twelfth hole during the final round of the British Open. Here he only could manage a bogey. But when he desperately needed a birdie on the sixteenth, he got it, and became the first man in forty years, and remains the only one since, to win the British Amateur and Open in one year.

13. Among the swirling of ticker tape, Jones the beloved hero rides up Broadway.

14. At City Hall in New York, Mayor Jimmy Walker greets Jones. "Here I am," said the affable mayor, "the worst golfer in the world introducing the best golfer in the world." Jones had only two weeks to prepare for the U.S. Open.

Old Course, Jones couldn't quite comprehend its sublime beauty. Actually, he hated it, but he was developing a respect for it, which is the cornerstone of any love.

After two rounds, Jones was still in the hunt, six strokes back with a total of 151. In the third round, a strong east wind whipped across the links. Jones took forty-six strokes on the front nine, and then on the tenth, a double bogey 6. Now his mood was as stormy as the winds that beat in from the fierce North Sea. On the short par-3 eleventh, Jones took five shots to reach the green. He then pocketed his ball and tore up his scorecard. He had quit in competition. It was an unforgivable breach of sportsmanship.

To the British it was plain sinful. The press severely criticized Jones, regarding his behavior as sacrilegious. Jones returned home, battered and confused. He knew he could never completely harness his temper, but he had to develop some moral outpost beyond which he would never go.

In that year's U.S. Amateur at the St. Louis Country Club, Jones's second-round opponent was Willie Hunter, the current British Amateur champion. It was a tight match. On the thirty-fifth hole, Hunter was only 1 up. It was still anyone's match. Hunter hit his pitch shot to the green, and Jones followed. He promptly skulled his approach over the green and flung his niblick. It bounced along the ground, then struck a woman in the leg. She was more surprised than hurt, but it was an unspeakable blow. Shaken, Jones lost the hole and the match.

The fact that he had come so very close to harming someone other than himself with his self-destructive temper was a stinging reality. When he returned to Atlanta, he received a letter from George Walker, then president of the USGA, and the man for whom the Walker Cup matches are named. He viewed Jones's club throwing with an uncompromising attitude, and at the end of the brief letter wrote, "You will never play in a USGA event again unless you can learn to control your temper."

Jones worried like a dog with an old bone. He still felt ashamed over his adolescent and stupid behavior at St. Andrews, and that coupled with his club throwing in the U.S. Amateur dredged up his worst fears. His temper was causing him to lose tournaments, but even worse, to be snubbed, rejected. For someone who had spent an infancy housebound, without a playmate, and for whom golf and friendship were an inseparable bond, it was worse than the most frightening nightmare.

Always the most merciless of critics when it came to his own golf game, Jones began to comprehend that he alone must take responsibility for his own actions. Six months after George Walker's letter, Jones got in touch with him to say he was trying to control his temper. Although during friendly rounds at East Lake Jones still flung his golf clubs, usually followed by a barrage of swear words, when it came to tournament golf he was like a reformed sinner. He set up the strictest code of sportsmanship for himself, from which he never wavered. Never again would he throw a club during a tournament; never again would he lose control of his temper in a tournament. He was beginning to learn that before one could be a champion one had to learn to lose gracefully. It was a hard fight he was winning—this being master of himself—and of it he wrote: "Golf may be . . . a sophisticated game. At least it is usually played with the outward appearance of great dignity. It is nevertheless a game of considerable passion, either of the explosive type or that which burns inwardly and sears the soul."

What subliminally had been running through Jones's unconscious now became a conscious reality: that while to him golf was a game of artful skill, it was, particularly played at its highest level, a test of character. In this final sense, the Grand Slam has few parallels in sport. . . .

7

Before Jones set out to capture the 1930 British Amateur, the only major national championship which he had yet to win, and the first domino that had to fall to set up the Grand Slam, Jones had one more vital task. He had to help win the Walker Cup matches for the United States. He was captain of the team for the second successive time, ranked as the finest golfer in the world. Yet, in a gesture so typical of his modesty, he placed himself only in the number-two position. This was the man who just six weeks before had beaten Gene Sarazen by twenty-seven strokes in the Southeastern Open. The number-one position on the team Jones assigned to Harrison Johnston, the reigning U.S. Amateur champion.

The Walker Cup matches were played on May 15 and 16 over the Royal St. George's Golf Club in Sandwich, on the southeastern coast of England. It was the sixth meeting between the best amateur golfers of the United States and the best of Great Britain and Ireland. As with the other five meetings, the United States won: the margin of victory was 10 to 2.

In the alternate-shot competition, Jones and his partner, Dr. O. F. Willing, won 8 and 7. The next day, in the singles competition, Jones's opponent was Roger Wethered, then considered the finest amateur golfer in England. Jones beat him 9 and 8.

The 1930 Walker Cup competition was the last in which Jones played. From the inaugural match played in 1922, Jones had played on five teams. (In 1923 he declined an invitation to play because it would have interfered with his studies at Harvard.) Jones's only loss occurred in the alternate shot competition in 1924. He won five successive singles matches, a record that has yet to be beaten, and his defeat of T. Philip Perkins of 13 and 12 in the 1928 matches is still a record.

Between the Walker Cup matches and the British Amateur, Jones played in an informal thirty-six-hole tournament at the Sunningdale Golf Club: *Golf Illustrated*'s Gold Vase. In the morning Jones shot a rather lackluster round of 75, placing him six shots behind the leader. He had let a certain lethargy of indifference get to him. The only way he felt he could get back into the tournament was to focus on the business at hand, and the only way he could do that was to have a little money riding on the afternoon round. He made a wager of a quid with a friend that he could break 70. It was an unusual gesture for Jones, who very rarely let his ego get the better of his wallet. But the wager did wonders. Jones shot a 68 for a tournament-record thirty-six-hole score of 143, and won the tournament. This he accomplished despite the fact that from time to time his mind kept running ahead to the British Amateur at St. Andrews and its seven grueling eighteen-hole matches, in which he knew anything could happen. Jones hated dipping, ever so slightly, into his reserve of nervous energy. He was going to need all he had, for not even the most imaginative dramatist could have conjured up more drama than Bobby Jones provided in the 1930 British Amateur.

At three o'clock Monday afternoon, May 26, a clear windless day, Jones faced his first opponent, an unknown golfer by the name of Henry Sidney Roper. An ex–coal miner from the Robin Hood district of Nottingham, and just one year younger than Jones, Roper was a man of medium height with a smooth, compact swing, a man who had gained a reputation as a fine long and mid-iron player. He had won the Nottingham Amateur four times.

As usual on the first tee, Jones shook hands with Roper and looked him straight in the eyes. Imemdiately, Jones got the impression that Roper was a man who played his best golf under pressure. And how right he was! Roper played the first five holes in five 4s. On the first green, Jones holed a long putt for a birdie 3. He parred the next hole, and birdied the third. On the long fourth, Jones's drive caught the famed bunker called "Cottage" down the left side of the fairway. He was 140 yards from the hourglass-shaped green. Jones studied the shot, took his spade-mashie (6-iron), and nipped the ball off the sand. It landed short of the green, rolled and rolled and rolled finally straight into the cup for an eagle. Jones birdied the next hole. After the first five holes he was five under par, but only 3 up. As Jones had expected on the first tee, Roper played very well under pressure: he showed no signs of cracking. In fact, Roper won the sixth hole. Jones won the seventh with a birdie and lost the eighth when he was laid a stymie. The ninth and tenth were halved; then Jones birdied the eleventh and twelfth and finally beat Roper on the sixteenth to win 3 and 2. In sixteen holes, Jones had scored six birdies and one eagle for a total of just sixty shots. As for Roper, he probably could have beaten anyone else but Jones that day; he had played every hole but the sixteenth in 4.

Jones had the next day off to rest. He had worked, suffered, and played brilliantly to beat Roper, and for the remaining days he was scheduled to play thirty-six holes each.

Wednesday, May 28, turned cold and windy. It was a fierce west wind—the most testing wind in which to play the Old Course. It blew with a near-gale force, whipping the heavy sand from the bunkers.

In the morning round that began at 8:15, Jones kept blowing on his hands to keep them warm. He defeated Cowan Shankland 5 and 3. Even though Jones played the front nine in forty shots, it wasn't Shankland's day; he four-putted the eighth and the eleventh.

May 28 was also a holiday in the nearby town of Dundee, and a larger-than-normal gallery, dressed in mittens and woolen waistcoats, followed the morning match. The gallery grew still larger in the afternoon as the near-gale winds continued to blow, for Jones's opponent was Cyril Tolley, a huge walrus of an Englishman, the defending British Amateur champion, a fierce competitor, and one of the longest drivers in the United Kingdom.

This was the match for which everyone in St. Andrews had waited, and it seemed as if every man, woman, and child in the town streamed onto the links. The mood of the gallery was so high-pitched with expectations that before the match there was an eerie stillness. It was the kind of afternoon when men instinctively speak in whispers.

The battle began at 1:35. Tolley drove first and topped his drive. It was the only mechanical error he made all day. Jones won the first hole; Tolley won the second. In the near-gale winds, both players had to be careful not to overdrive the greens playing downwind on the 300-yard-plus holes. Tolley drove the ninth green 306 yards from the tee; on the twelfth, 314 yards, both Jones and Tolley overdrove the green. Balls would fly up to the green into the wind and then be blown back. At the core, it was a match to test one's resourcefulness.

Thrust and parry followed each player as quickly as lightning. The lead changed hands three times, with neither player gaining more than a 1-up lead. At the thirteenth, Jones holed a beautiful 36-foot putt for a birdie to go 1 up. On the 512-yard, par-5 fourteenth, Tolley put his second shot within a yard of the hole pin. An eagle. Jones came back at the fifteenth putting his second shot to within five feet of the pin. A birdie to go 1 up. On the sixteenth, Jones drove into a fairway bunker known as the "Principal's Nose," pitched out, and took a bogey 5 to Tolley's par. Now the match was even with two holes to play.

The par-5 seventeenth, the "Road Hole" as it is called, is a slight dogleg right, with out-of-bounds down the right side, and a green of inglorious security, protected by a deep bunker on its left side and a road almost hugging its right side. Both Jones and Tolley drove down the left side of the fairway, not daring to flirt with the out-of-bounds right. Having driven farther left than Tolley, Jones was away. He studied the shot for a long time; he was coming into the narrow green on the bias. If he used the wrong club, or hit the wrong shot, surely he would either be in the vicious bunker or on the road, and from either place it would be almost impossible to get down in two. He finally elected to go for the green in two with a mid-mashie (a 4-iron). The shot he selected to play was part of his golfing genius. He aimed for the upper-left portion of the green; if he missed he would be left with an easy pitch to the green. The shot didn't come off. The ball cleared the bunker, then took an awful kick left. Fate smiled on Jones; his ball hit a spectator, and came to rest on the back fringe of the green.

Tolley played short of the green with his second, then hit an exquisite pitch shot—the kind of shot that wins championships. The ball rolled slowly through the small swales of the green and stopped two feet from the pin. Jones's chip was weak, stopping eight feet from the hole. Jones knew the round, the match, the tournament, rested on the 8-foot putt. His putter, Calamity Jane, proved, indeed, to be more piercing than a needle's point. Jones holed the putt. In a way, Jones's putt could have been eighty feet. Tolley holed his putt.

Down the eighteenth, both drove within thirty feet of the green. Jones hit a pitch-and-run shot through the big swale in front of the green, judiciously called the "Valley of Sin." It was the proper shot but a shade strong, and the ball rolled twenty-five feet past the pin. Tolley's shot finished twelve feet short of the pin. Jones putted carefully to within a few inches of the cup for a par. He then stood by, feeling an impotent agony as he watched Tolley line up his birdie putt that would end the match. Tolley missed.

Off the two valiant warriors went to the first hole of sudden death. Both hit good drives. Jones's second shot was a beauty, stopping ten feet from the pin. Tolley overshot the green and chipped back poorly, leaving himself a nasty 7-foot putt. Since Jones could only lose the hole by three-putting, he ever so carefully putted the ball so close to the pin that his next putt would be conceded; but even better, he laid Tolley a stymie. The big Englishman failed to negotiate it.

The duel was over. Jones felt he had fought a battle with broadswords. Later he wrote of the match, "I was neither exultant nor elated, just very, very tired. I suspected that Cyril felt the same way."

Had it been Jones who had to jump the stymie at the nine-teenth, he probably would have negotiated it beautifully. While Jones sometimes felt fatalistic about golf tournaments, a kind of come-what-may attitude, this time it was somehow different. He felt he was destined to win the British Amateur. Simply, he felt he could not lose. O. B. Keeler began sharing Jones's view, for in the match against Tolley, Jones had been outplayed but had gotten the breaks. And after two other tight battles, both Jones and Keeler were convinced that a Providence wouldn't let Jones lose.

It was a queer feeling, with deep ironic overtones, particu-larly because it was felt in a town named after the Christian martyr Andrew, a fisherman in the Sea of Galilee and one of the first Apostles called by Jesus. The St. Andrew's cross, white against a blue background, is the national symbol of Scotland.

On May 29, the fierce west wind had lessened and shifted, and now was only a puff of zephyr winds. In the morning, Jones beat another Englishman. G. O. Watt, 7 and 6, playing twelve holes in forty-five strokes.

That afternoon, Jones faced Harrison Johnston, the U.S. Amateur champion. Johnston's game was getting sharper each day. Only in the first round had he been pushed, and then by none other than the great golf writer, Bernard Darwin. The match had been all even coming to the famed seventeenth hole. Johnston went for the green in two, and laced a beautiful spoon shot, the ball ending up a mere yard from the pin. That was the match.

Even Darwin, who at times could be the harshest of critics (he once looked at a man's tie and said to him, "I say, is that your school tie or your unfortunate bad taste?"), had to praise Johnston, though it took him three long paragraphs in his column in *The Times* (London) to work up to it. Of that spoon shot at the seventeenth, he wrote: "There was no answer possible to such a thrust. That was the match, and the stroke was so audacious and so perfectly struck that any grudging criticism is out of the question."

Against Johnston, Jones played wonderful, consistent golf, playing the first seven holes in seven 4s. He was 2 up at the end of nine, and after the thirteenth was 4 up. Then Johnston, noted for his heroic finishes, put on a charge. (In 1924 he had won the Western Amateur after being 5 down with six holes to play.) Johnston won the fourteenth with a birdie, and the fifteenth when Jones three-putted. At the sixteenth, Johnston had to hole a tricky 12-foot putt to stay in the match. He holed it. He won the seventeenth, again reaching the green in two. Jones was only 1 up. He had lost three holes and made only one mistake. Both men reached the eighteenth green safely, but Johnston was ninety feet from the pin, and Jones half that distance. Johnston then stroked a beautiful putt. The ball rolled and rolled across the huge, slick green, dipping and turning, going straight for the cup as if being pulled by a magical magnet. The ball stopped two inches short.

Jones hit a poor putt, a stroke that was like an afterthought. He left himself a tricky 8-foot sidehill putt to avoid going into extra holes. Again, the putt could have been eighty feet. That eerie feeling that a certain Providence was with Jones was stronger than ever. He holed the putt.

On Friday, May 30, a windless but very chilly day, Jones played Eric Fidden in the morning. After eight holes, he was one under even 4s, 4 up. He played par golf the remaining holes and won 4 and 3.

Before his afternoon match, the semi-finals, against his United States Walker Cup teammate, George Voigt, Jones had a long wait. He had a leisurely lunch with his wife, then relaxed with her in his living room of the Grand Hotel overlooking the eighteenth green, sipping a glass of sherry. While Jones had more than a normal tolerance for whiskey, sherry was a different thing. His face flushed and his depth perception was thrown off.

On the first hole, Voigt, wearing woolen mittens with half-cut-off fingers and a heavy Shetland sweater, holed a 15-foot putt for a birdie. Jones, only twelve feet from the pin, knew he was in for another battle. He holed his putt, but it was the only putt of any significant length he would make for the next two hours. Some wonderful, nameless music had gone out of his putting stroke. The aggregate total of putts Jones missed was criminal. On the fifth and seventh holes, he missed putts of under four feet. He couldn't continue with impunity.

Voigt, on the other hand, was playing one of the best rounds of his life, consistently sticking his iron shots inside of Jones's on the green. At the end of the tenth hole, the match was even. Voigt won the eleventh when Jones overshot the green. On the par-4 thirteenth, Voigt hit a beautiful drive into the crosswind, just light of a huge hollow called the "Lion's Mouth." He then pitched to within two feet of the pin, making his 3 to Jones's 4. Jones was now 2 down with five holes to play.

Darwin, who was watching the match, felt that the only way Jones was going to win was to have the match handed to him, and handed to him it was. On the fourteenth, Voigt misjudged the strength of the crosswind and drove out-of-bounds. Jones got his par. Now he was only 1 down. The fifteenth was halved. At the sixteenth, Voigt again misjudged the crosswind and drove into that strangely called bunker, the "Principal's Nose." Jones won the hole and squared the match.

On the seventeenth, Voigt waged a brave counterattack,

and despite the crosswind, he went for the green in two. The ball stopped on the front edge of the green. Jones, who had played safely short with his second shot, pitched eighteen feet past the pin. Voigt struck a splendid putt, with the ball pulling up only eight inches short of the cup. He had his birdie. To halve the hole, Jones had to sink his 18-foot putt. He studied the putt and saw the line as clearly as if it had been drawn by the Lord. He holed the putt—as he knew he would.

At the eighteenth, a shaken Voigt committed a cardinal error, trying to pitch the ball just over the front mound. The stroke was a shade light, and the ball rolled into the "Valley of Sin." Jones's pitch was eight feet right of the pin. Voigt chipped to within six feet of the pin. Compared to his putt on the seventeenth, Jones now faced a comparatively easy putt to end the match. He missed it, but got his par. To halve the hole, Voigt had to make his 6-footer, but like Tolley and Johnston before him, he missed. Jones had won, and went to the clubhouse more dead than alive. For the third time in three days, Jones had won by the narrowest of margins: 1 up.

Jones's opponent in the finals was Roger Wethered, who faced the almost hopeless task of trying to keep up with a fiercely determined Jones. With all fairness to Wethered, at this point Bobby Jones could probably have stopped even General Sherman's march to the sea.

On Saturday, May 31, 15,000 Scots jammed onto the Old Course to see Jones. He gave them a terrible fright when, on the first hole, he missed his second shot so badly the ball not only didn't come close to the green but fell short of the Swilcan Burn, a creek running in front of the green. Then Jones hit a lovely pitch and one-putted for his four. Over the next fifteen holes, Jones played almost flawless golf; he had made nothing higher than a 4. At the seventeenth, he stood 5 up. He went for the green in two, and for the first time all week his ball landed in the treacherous Road Bunker left of the green. With just the briefest hesitation, Jones marched into the bunker with his niblick and popped the ball out; it landed on the edge of the green and rolled slowly four feet past the pin. Then, after Wethered got down a tricky putt for a birdie 4, Jones stepped up for his simple 4-footer, knowing he couldn't miss. He did. Both players parred the eighteenth.

Francis Ouimet, who walked back to the Grand Hotel with Jones at lunchtime, couldn't understand it when Jones started pacing angrily around his living room.

"Bob, what in the world has gotten into you? You're four up."

"Did you hear what that official said on the first tee?" Jones asked.

Ouimet pondered the question, and then remembered that before the match, the official had said that in all the years, none of the greatest golfers in the world ever had played the Old Course without taking a five.

"And Goddamnit," said Jones, "I had to go and miss a damn four-foot putt to miss my four and to miss being the first man who ever played St. Andrews without taking a five."

Jones had taken a silly conversational point and turned it into a personal challenge. He had been playing the Old Course instead of Wethered.

Then promptly on the first hole of the afternoon round, Jones three-putted and took a five. But that was about the only mistake he made. Smelling victory, he played a neat mixture of cautious and aggressive golf. Wethered started to spray his drives and missed several short putts. When Jones rolled in a 3-foot putt on the twelfth hole, the thirtieth of the match, he had beaten Wethered 7 and 6.

107

And how the Scots loved it. At that moment, no one could have called a Scot dour. Shouting and cheering, they converged on Jones like a swarm of locusts. Jones had to be escorted back to the clubhouse by four constables. A band that was supposed to have played the victor in near the eighteenth was scattered in the stampede and never got to play a note. When O. B. Keeler finally reached Jones, the champion put his arm around his Boswell's shoulder and said, "O. B., honestly, I don't care what happens now. I'd rather have won this tournament than anything else in golf. I'm satisfied." Jones had told Keeler almost the same thing after he had won his first championship, the 1923 U.S. Open.

Everyone in Scotland, perhaps even in all of Great Britain, felt the best player had won the 1930 British Amateur, and their feelings were statistically backed up. In five days of play, some of it in near-gale winds, Jones scored only two double bogeys. A scorekeeper noted that Jones had the distinction of returning the best card for the round in each round of play in which he took part. In other words, matching cards at the finish of each round, Jones would have proved the winner over any of the other 167 competitors. Jones had played 143 holes of golf in six under even 4s.

For a while Jones basked in his triumph, going to Paris to celebrate with Mary and some friends. Then suddenly, before he truly had time to get mentally prepared, the British Open loomed like a hurdle to a hurdler off his stride. Jones, a man for whom readiness was all, struggled to dust out the mental cobwebs, and perfect his game. He confessed all the while that he was never quite sure where the ball was going after he hit it. And this time he didn't feel there was a mysterious presence walking with him.

Of all his tournaments that year, Jones played his sloppiest golf in the British Open at Hoylake, The Royal Liverpool Golf Club. It's a long course hugging the Irish Sea just outside Liverpool near the estuary where, in the seventeenth century, William of Orange sheltered his fleet before the Battle of Boyne.

Jones's victory in the British Open was both a test of the resolution of his character and a testimony to one of the things it had taken him so long to learn. During Jones's "seven lean years," the fine pro Jim Barnes had told Jones, "Bob, you can't always be playing well when it counts. You'll never win golf tournaments until you learn to score well when you're playing badly."

Jones qualified for the British Open with scores of 73 and 77 for a total of 150, which tied him with six other players for twentieth place, among 296 entrants.

On June 18, a warm sultry morning with storm clouds moving in slowly across the Irish Sea, Jones began his quest for his second major championship, trying to become the first American and the first golfer in forty years (since England's John Ball did it in 1890) to capture both the British Amateur and Open championships in a single year.

The first three holes at Hoylake consist of two shortish par-4s, and a par-5 very reachable in two—not a very difficult stretch, and like the rest of the course lacking in any subtlety. Yet it was on these holes where Jones almost lost the Open. In the first three rounds, he played them in five over par or eight over even 4s. Compared to how he had played 143 holes over the Old Course in six under even 4s, Jones was far from being in championship form.

Jones was also playing the course contrary to the rest of the field, who were picking up strokes on par on the first three holes, then losing them on the last five, a brutal stretch of two par-5s and three par-4s measuring 2,318 yards, or 457 yards per hole. In the first three rounds, Jones played them in only one over par.

After the first round, Jones led with a two-under-par 70, which included six 3s. "It was," Jones said, "one of the hardest rounds I have had to play, and as I always have one in each tournament, I hope it is over and done with." It wasn't. Jones had chipped and putted beautifully; as he said wryly of the perfect conditions of the greens, "Their only fault is that they give no possible excuse for a missed putt."

Jones's second round was an even par 72, and he maintained his slim one-shot lead over the English pro Fred Robson; three over Horton Smith; and five over Archie Compston, a tall, rugged-looking Englishman with a confident stride who had once taught the Prince of Wales. Macdonald Smith and another American, Leo Diegel, were six strokes back.

At just past 9:30 on Saturday, June 20, a cloudless brisk day with a slight breeze coming in from the Irish Sea, Jones began his final two rounds. He wore his favorite brown-and-white shoes, gray woolen knickers, a white shirt, and a pale blue cashmere sweater. He played the first three holes in two over par, going 4, 5, and 6, but made a par 3 on the next. An hour later, Compston played the same holes in 4, 3, 4, and 2. In four holes he had wiped out Jones's five-shot lead over him. Quite simply, Compston was playing inspired golf and Jones wasn't. Jones played the last five holes poorly, taking four 5s and one 4, finishing with a 74.

In the clubhouse, before his afternoon round, Jones was having a ham sandwich and tea, and could see Compston. Jones later wrote of the scene, "He was truly striding after the ball as though he could not wait to vent his fury upon it. Watching, I saw him sweep past the sixteenth green. I had the feeling that spectators, tee boxes, benches even might be swirled up into his wake. As he left the eighteenth green, after his great 68, and made his beaming way to the clubhouse through a myriad of well-wishers, he was about as happy a figure as I have ever seen. At the time, I was heading for the first tee to start my final round." Compston now led Jones by a stroke.

Now the sky was slowly blackening and a fine mist was falling, perfect weather for a man to hear stealthy footsteps behind him. Jones faced those first three holes he had come to fear. On the first he got an easy par. His drive on the second was a high howling push. The ball landed right on the top of the head of a gallery steward, then careened fifty yards into a bunker guarding the fourteenth green. Miraculously, the steward wasn't injured by the blow, and Jones's ball was lying cleanly in the bunker 120 yards from the green. He then smacked the ball twenty feet from the pin, and holed the putt for a birdie 3, a score that should have been a bogey. It was the kind of turnaround that can snap a player's game into shape, and that's just what it did for Jones. He parred the next hole and, although he bogeyed the fourth, he then clicked off three neat pars. On the long par-5 eighth, Jones's second shot just missed the green and rolled down a small bank fifteen yards away. Jones, surely as the clouds were still blackening, was going for a birdie. Describing what then happened, Bernard Darwin wrote in *The Times* (London) that "a nice old lady with a croquet mallet could have saved Jones two strokes."

The pin was placed fifteen feet from the edge of the green. Jones played his third shot, a chip to the edge of the green, but the shot was weakly played and the ball failed to reach the putting surface. Then, as error breeds error, Jones's second chip was weak, leaving him a 10-foot putt for a par. Trying

111

desperately not to lose any more strokes, Jones putted boldly and slipped the ball by the hole, less than two feet. He then hurriedly went to tap the ball in and missed. An easy birdie had turned into a double bogey. A muted electricity ran through the gallery.

Jones was dazed, as if he had been a boxer suddenly hit by a thunderous right cross that seemed to come from nowhere.

Now he played with the bit of fear between his teeth. He steadied his frayed nerves as best he could. Like a wounded battler, his fierce fighting instincts became more intense, as did his will to win. Somehow, he parred the ninth, and posted a front nine of 38.

Jones's pale blue-gray eyes were stormy in concentration as he played the next five holes in even 4s, with two bogeys, one birdie, and two pars. He bogeyed the fifteenth when he failed to sink an 8-foot putt for a par. Instinctively, he knew that if there was still the faintest chance of winning the championship, he needed to birdie the sixteenth, a par 5 of 532 yards with the fairway doglegging right around an open field: an out-of-bounds.

Jones hit a perfect drive down the right center of the fairway, then went for the green with a brassie. He pulled the shot. The ball bounced into the sandy bank of a bunker left of the green. Jones examined the shot for a long time and realized he could not take a normal full backswing. The ball had to get up quickly in order to clear the lip of the bunker. He elected to play the shot with a concave wedge, a club given to him by Horton Smith during the Savannah Open that spring. Jones had never before hit any shot of consequence with the club, and here he faced a crucial shot, one in which he possibly could win the championship.

With his right foot almost on top of the bank and his body

coiled over so that he was almost at eye level with the green, Jones hit down on the ball with a sharp descending blow, catching less than an inch of sand before the ball. Up popped the ball, easily clearing the lip of the bunker. It rolled lazily across the slick green and stopped two inches from the cup. If ever an explosion shot was heard around the world, that one was. Jones got his birdie. He parred the last two holes and posted a 75, three over par. His total was 291, three over even 4s and ten strokes better than Walter Hagen when he had won the British Open at Hoylake in 1924.

Now all Jones could do was wait for the other competitors to play their rounds. Never had the hands crawled so slowly around the face of a clock. To calm himself, Jones had a stiff whiskey and water, but his right hand trembled too much for him even to hold the glass. Finally, he cupped the glass with both hands and downed it quickly. He had another and waited.

Already, Compston had faded. On the very first hole that afternoon, he missed an 18-inch putt for a par, which broke the spine of his spirit. He needed fourteen more strokes that afternoon than he had taken that morning to get around the course. He finally posted an 82.

But two American pros, Leo Diegel and Macdonald Smith, playing an hour behind Jones, were very much in the hunt. Diegel came to the sixteenth tee needing to par the last three holes to tie Jones. A birdie on one would win the championship. His drive on the sixteenth caught the fairway bunker. His third to the green caught a green-side bunker. He took a bogey 6, and that was it for Diegel.

Macdonald Smith had to play the last five holes in one under even 4s to tie—an impossible task. But Smith was a gamey golfer with a beautiful and graceful swing. He had a peculiarity of never taking divots; instead, he just sort of brushed the ball off the turf, as though, in the words of Tommy Armour, "it were an altar cloth."

He made a par at the fourteenth, but he had needed a birdie. While his task was almost hopeless, he did try. He picked up a beautiful birdie at the sixteenth, and then parred the seventeenth. After a perfect drive down the eighteenth fairway, he needed to hole his approach shot to tie Jones. He sent a steward ahead to tend the pin. Jones watched, his hands cupped around a glass of whiskey and water. Smith's ball came sailing up beautifully to the green, bounced in front of the cup, and ran past. Jones slowly removed his left hand from his glass.

PART THREE

The U.S. Open

8

On Wednesday, July 2, 1930, Bobby Jones, the only American golfer ever to capture the British Amateur and Open championships in one year, arrived in New York City aboard the S.S. *Europa*. He was given the hero's welcome: the traditional ticker-tape parade.

At 4:00 P.M. that afternoon—a hot, humid day in the city, the kind when you can see heat shimmering off the pavement—the parade began from the Battery up Broadway. Beneath a blizzard of swirling ticker tape, preceded by seventy mounted policemen, and with a band playing "Valencia," the motorcade slowly wound its way up the narrow street. Thousands of spectators packed the sidewalks, as they had in 1926 for Gertrude Ederle, the first woman to swim the English Channel, and in 1927 for Charles Lindbergh. Jones wore the chaplet of a peaceful conquest. The channel he had crossed had been the Atlantic Ocean, and his plane had been a steep pitch to a small patch of green.

That day had been an unusually quiet one in the financial district. The brokers and traders were now working only five-hour days, and July 2 had been the slowest trading day in more than two years, with a mere 1.3 million shares of stocks being traded. One broker who didn't know about the parade approached a massive policeman, worrying and sweating profusely, and asked, "What's the parade for?" The policeman replied disgustedly, "Oh, for some God damn golf player!"

The shy and modest Jones was suffering and sweating just about as much as the policeman. Behind his broad, thankful smile was a grimace.

At 5:00 P.M. the motorcade reached City Hall Plaza, and Mayor Jimmy Walker greeted Jones. "Here you are, the greatest golfer in the world being introduced by the worst one."

Two hundred and fifty Atlantans who had taken a train called the "Bobby Jones Special" to New York City yelled in unison, "Atta boy, Jimmy."

That evening there was a dinner honoring Jones given by 400 of his closest friends at the Vanderbilt Hotel. The next day, Jones, his father and mother, and scores of friends left for Minneapolis aboard the Twentieth Century. The U.S. Open at the Interlachen Country Club, eight miles west of Minneapolis, would begin in seven days. Jones's wife, Mary, was returning to Atlanta to take care of their two children—Clara, age five, and Robert Tyre Jones III, age three. The boy had sent up a very important message to his father: "Tell Daddy I can whistle now."

Jones had only a few days to prepare for the U.S. Open, and this was during a scorching heat wave then gripping the Midwest. Jones worked on his timing. He was trying to coalesce those hundreds of elements that made up his beautiful and graceful long swing. The 6,672-yard course was set over rolling terrain with five lakes, smallish greens, and an almost knee-high rough which would be the mightiest foe for the golfers. Two days before the championship, Jones shot a two-under-par 70.

After the round, Jones said, "That was the first time since the Southeastern Open in Augusta that everything felt just right."

Walter Hagen felt he was playing well, but still needed a little more practice. And he was exceedingly pleased with a new set of clubs. For the first time in a major championship, The Haig was playing with steel-shafted clubs. The consensus of the players was that the winning score would be 292, four over par.

On Thursday, July 10, the U.S. Open began. The temperature in the shade registered over ninety-five degrees, and the humidity was almost as high. Jones started off at 9:45. He played the front nine in a neat 34 shots; he played the back nine, in the hottest heat of the day, in just less than an hour and a half and 37 strokes. His score, a neat 71, stood as the lowest of the day until late that afternoon when Macdonald Smith and Tommy Armour both posted 70s.

So intense was the heat that Armour rubbed his face and forehead with a pack of ice before each shot. Ed Dudley and Chick Evans experienced spells of dizziness. Jim Barnes walked beneath a large green umbrella. Hagen, who never played with a hat, simply because he got paid handsomely for endorsing a particular hair tonic, stated that he wouldn't stir the next day without a big straw hat.

For those who might wonder where dignity goes when it melts, there was Cyril Tolley. The big seal of an Englishman, who had given Jones such a fierce battle in the British Amateur in near-gale winds, lost nine pounds that first day. A woman watching him walk slowly up a hill, his clothes soaked with perspiration, said, "Mr. Tolley looks like an iceman who has carried one hundred pounds of ice up five flights of stairs and found that the lady of the house was not at home." Tolley shot an 80.

Jones had dressed in light gray knickers, a white cap, a white shirt, and a red foulard tie. He carried a half dozen red-colored tees in his pocket. After his round, his knickers were so saturated with perspiration they were almost black, and the red tees had stained one leg of his knickers. His red tie had run all over his shirt.

The next day brought a cooling eastern breeze, and the humidity dropped; now the temperature was only in the low nineties. Jones played the front nine almost exactly as he had the first day, except for a bogey 5 on the long first hole, a 478-yard par 4, and a birdie 2 on the par-3 fifth.

On the ninth, a 485-yard par 5 with a big blue lake in front of the green, Jones hit the most controversial shot of the tournament. After a long drive down the right side of the fairway, Jones faced a spoon shot to reach the green. In practice and in the first round, he had reached the green easily and made birdies.

As usual, there were more than 8,000 spectators; Jones literally was hitting down a human alleyway. Just as Jones reached the top of his backswing, his eye caught a sharp movement in the gallery—two little girls were running ahead—and instinctively he flinched. He half-topped his shot. The ball took off in a low trajectory and didn't climb. It was heading straight for the lake. Now the best Jones could hope for was a bogey. But when the ball hit the water, it skipped twice and landed on the bank. From there Jones pitched to within four feet of the pin and holed his putt for a birdie.

15. Jones and his chief rival, Walter Hagen, before their epic duel in the winter of 1926. The Haig, or Sir Walter, as he was called, had a record second only to Jones's: he won eleven major championships, including two U.S. Opens, five P.G.A. Championships and four British Opens.

16. During a warm-up round for the 1926 Walker Cup matches: Jess Guilford, Francis Ouimet, Bobby Jones, and Watts Gunn.

17.   Qualifying for the 1926 British Open at Sunningdale Golf Club in England, Jones stunned the gallery with one of the greatest rounds of golf ever played. In carving a symmetrically beautiful 66, Jones hit every green but one in or under regulation figures, and on every par 5 was putting for an eagle. He made only 3s and 4s, hit 33 shots, stroked 33 putts, went out in 33, and came in in 33.

18.   The reception ship *Macom* greets Jones in New York City in 1926 after he won his first of three British Opens.

19. Up from Atlanta welcoming Jones was his family. Left to right: his father, "The Colonel"; his mother, Clara; his wife, Mary; and his paternal grandparents. The man on the far right is Robert Tyre Jones, for whom Bobby Jones was named.

20. Bob and Mary on deck of the *Macom* before the ticker-tape parade up Broadway.

21. By his own admission, this remained Jones's favorite photograph of himself. He is holding the U.S. Amateur trophy after beating Chick Evans 8 and 7 to take the 1927 U.S. Amateur, a championship Jones would win a record five times.

22.   One of the most crucial putts Jones ever holed, a 12-foot sidehill putt on the final green at Winged Foot Golf Club during the 1929 U.S. Open. After frittering away a huge lead, Jones needed to hole this putt to tie Al Espinosa. In the play-off, Jones beat Espinosa by twenty-three shots.

23.   Jones felt the terrible strain of championship golf so severely at times that during a championship he often lost from twelve to eighteen pounds.

For more than twenty-five years, until Jones denied it, the spoon shot was known as the "lily pad shot," because thousands of spectators claimed Jones's ball had actually struck a lily pad and then skidded onto the bank. There was no lily pad involved. With its low trajectory and the force with which it hit the water, the ball came in precisely like a flat stone being skipped across the surface. For sure, it was a stroke of luck, but in this championship, luck would even out. The unluckiest blow came at the worst possible juncture.

Jones played the back nine in 39, three over par. He bogeyed the seventeenth, the longest par 3 in U.S. Open history. It was a mean golf hole of 262 yards that called for a precise drive or brassie shot to a small green guarded on either side by bunkers. The right side of the fairway up to and beyond the green sloped toward a lake. In the whole tournament, only two birdies were made on the hole, one by Walter Hagen. The hole had a weird effect on Jones, one almost as strangely instinctive as that on a horse wanting to return to a burning barn. During the championship, Jones played the seventeenth in four over par.

At the end of the second round, Horton Smith, with a total of 142, led Jones by only two shots, hardly a very safe margin. Within five shots of the leader were four former U.S. Open champions: Jones, Tommy Armour, Johnny Farrell, and Walter Hagen. Collectively, they had won twenty-four major championships.

On Saturday morning, with thirty-six holes scheduled, the USGA posted a sign: "Play-off thirty-six holes 10 A.M. and 2 P.M. Sunday." It was a likely forecast. The last three U.S. Opens had been decided by play-offs. Jones had been involved in two.

For two days Jones had played well within himself. Not

being the leader, he wasn't, as he would later write, "oppressed by that feeling of having something to protect." His tactic was to break quickly from the pack. Except for the mean seventeenth, there wasn't a hole that had him baffled.

Jones's third round was almost a perfect fusion of his mental and physical powers. Except for a slight faltering on the last two holes, the round was brilliant. Jones burned with a gem-like flame. He missed only three greens in regulation figures and only three fairways. He had nine one-putt greens; the longest putt he holed was a 10-footer on the first hole, and in all he took only twenty-seven putts. He scored six birdies, ten pars, and two bogeys. So accurate was his play with the mashie niblick (7-iron) that the aggregate distance the ball stopped from the pin was more measurable in inches than feet. His three shots with the club put the ball an average of thirty inches from the pin.

Jones also had the psychological edge on the field, now cut from 143 starters (there were 1,177 entries) to 66, by having an early starting time: 9:15. As Jones made birdie after birdie, the cheers from his huge gallery echoed across the course. It had an almost devastating effect on the other players. They started to press. On the sixth, Walter Hagen three-putted from four feet. And then there was poor Willie MacFarlane, not quite out of it, nine strokes off the lead at the start of the third round, who three-putted four greens in a row and eleven in all to post a third round total of 82.

After Jones holed his 10-footer at the long first hole for a par, he clicked off two more pars. Then on the par-5 fourth, Jones faced a delicate third shot, a pitch over a bunker to a green sloping steeply away from him to the pin, itself placed less than fifteen feet from the bunker. With the touch of a hairdresser, Jones played the pitch perfectly, landing the ball just over the bunker on the edge of the green and letting it slowly run down the slope. It ended four feet past the pin. A birdie. Jones easily parred the fifth. Then came the crescendo. On the sixth, Jones faced a second shot to an elevated green guarded by steep-walled bunkers. Out came the mashie niblick. The ball flew straight toward the pin and stopped twenty-three inches away. Again a birdie. On the next hole, from the rough, another mashie-niblick shot; this time the ball stopped five feet from the pin. Another birdie. He finished with two pars for a 33.

He parred the tenth, made two birdies at the back-to-back par 5s, the eleventh and twelfth, then three more pars. At the par-4 sixteenth, Jones's second shot was another mashie niblick. Again the ball went straight at the pin and dropped as softly as a grapefruit six inches from the pin. Another birdie. Two pars would give Jones a 66, a record U.S. Open round; but on the seventeenth, his brassie tee shot caught the right-side bunker, and after a poor explosion shot, he failed to get down a 14-foot putt for his par. He bogeyed the eighteenth after badly slicing his drive. He posted a 68, still the lowest round of the tournament.

The field not only backed off from Jones, but from par. There were only two other sub-par rounds that morning. Horton Smith and Walter Hagen slipped to 76s. Tommy Armour posted a 75. Jones led by five shots. Now it was no longer anyone's championship; it was Jones's. At least, so it appeared once again. But then, Jones so often had seemed to have won so many Opens.

9

Ironically, Jones played in his first U.S. Open when his idol, the great English professional, Harry Vardon, played in his last—in 1920 at the Inverness Club in Toledo, Ohio. Jones was eighteen. Vardon was fifty. For more than a quarter of a century, Vardon had been playing championship golf, having won his first British Open in 1896.

Unquestionably, no golfer was more ahead of his time technically than Vardon. The overlapping grip that he employed and popularized became the grip of the future (it is still known as the Vardon grip); his upright swing (though his left arm was quite bent at the top of the backswing) became the swing of the future. His modified hip turn, especially with his iron play, became the pivot of the future. The way he hit the ball, with a beautiful controlled fade, became the shot of the future. Vardon was doing all these things before 1910.

The 1920 U.S. Open is remembered more as the one that Vardon lost, slipping seven strokes over par over the last seven holes, than as the one his English sidekick, the long-hitting, pipe-smoking Ted Ray, won by a single stroke.

From the very beginning, the shades of drama were raised with that eternal shifting of the rising and falling star. In the qualifying rounds, Jones was paired with Vardon.

The youngster played himself into contention with a third-round 70, the second-lowest round of the championship. He didn't know then that a contender cracks in either the third or fourth round. Before the final round, Jones finished off his lunch with his usual large helpings of apple pie and ice cream. If only he had known how very close he was to winning. An even par round would have won him the Open; a round of one over would have put him into a play-off. Jones started his last round filled with apple pie, ice cream, and inexperience. He gambled for birdies, but instead got bogeys, and finished with a 77, eventually placing him in a tie for eighth place.

As disappointing as Jones's final round was, nothing could equal the tragic finish of Harry Vardon, who always played in a sort of self-hypnotic state, his face cast in the mask of the wise philosopher. After a birdie at the eleventh, he could take as many as forty-one strokes and win. As he reached the twelfth tee, a windstorm suddenly whipped in off Lake Erie. The strong winds came whining across the fairways; the inky-black clouds were thick with curses. Playing into the teeth of the wind, it took Vardon four shots to reach the green on the 522-yard par 5, plus two putts. A 6. He missed a 2-foot putt for a par on the thirteenth. He three-putted the next three holes, and on the par-3 seventeenth, now weary and looking more like a man of seventy, Vardon put his second shot into the brook in front of the green, and that was it. He had stumbled to a final round of 78. The wind, the cleanest of all hazards in golf, had bowed the head of the aging lion.

The 1921 U.S. Open was won by Jim Barnes, a tall immigrant from Cornwall who, when he bent over a putt, looked like a large question mark. Jones played himself completely out of contention in the third round, taking forty putts, the most he took in any U.S. Open. He finished tied for fifth. That was when Walter Hagen prophesied that Jones would win the Open before he won the Amateur. Jones thought The Haig was joking.

The next year in the 1922 Open, the first time the USGA charged spectators an admission fee of one dollar, Jones almost made Hagen's prophecy come true. Starting the final round, he was tied for the lead. He felt a final round 68 would win the championship, and it did. But the player who scored it was a small knot of a man, five feet five inches tall with black hair and a swarthy complexion, and only twenty years old, from Harrison, New York. His name was Gene Sarazen (actually, he had changed his last name from Saraceni, which he felt sounded like a violinist). Being four strokes off the pace, he had started his round an hour and a half before the leaders. At the third hole, he sank a 40-foot putt for a birdie; on the next hole, a 25-footer for a birdie. He collected another birdie at the fourteenth. At the 500-yard, par-5 eighteenth, he needed to hit a driver off the fairway to reach the green. He two-putted. Another birdie and a 68 made a total of 288. When a friend found Sarazen sitting alone on a rail fence, and told him several other players were making a run at his 288, Sarazen brashly replied, "I've got mine. Let them get theirs." No one did.

Jones finished tied for second, failing to finish with two 4s, but for the first time since 1916 he had beaten out Chick Evans as the low amateur. Seemingly it was a small consolation, but the rivalry between Jones and Evans had now become a bitter one. At last, Jones was rightfully acclaimed as the finest amateur golfer in the country; that honor would be briefly enjoyed.

Six weeks later, Jones reached the semi-finals of the U.S. Amateur played at The Country Club in the Boston suburb of Brookline, Massachusetts. He got the worst beating of his career over thirty-six holes by Jess Sweetser, who won 8 and 7. Jones was not playing well; Sweetser was playing magnificently. At the start of the afternoon round, Jones was 7 down, but still in a fighting mood. On the second hole, Sweetser holed a pitch shot of eighty yards for an eagle. The best Jones could do for a halve was to hole his pitch. His ball stopped six inches from the pin.

After the match Sweetser said, "Well, Bob, I've beaten the best man in the field."

The next day, Sweetser beat Chick Evans and won his first and only U.S. Amateur.

The defeat was more than unusually painful to Jones, for he would be spending most of the next two years in neighboring Cambridge at Harvard University.

On June 6, 1922, Jones had graduated in the top third of his class at the Georgia School of Technology (Georgia Tech) with a Bachelor of Science degree in mechanical engineering. In four years of mathematics he averaged 97; in four years of chemistry, 87; in two years of English he scored two 90s. He had a 97 in geology and 85s in both physics and electrical engineering. He scored consistently in the high 70s in his major, mechanical engineering.

In the yearbook, *The Blue Print*, the following was written beneath a small photo of Jones: "Yes, this is none other than the famous Bob of golfing fame. We can't tell you too much about him that you don't already know unless that he's a darn good student as well as a golfer, not to mention he is exceedingly popular with his fellow students."

Jones was voted the second most popular man in his class, the first being George Griffin, who from 1945 to 1964 served as Dean of Students of Georgia Tech.

On September 25, 1922, Bobby Jones entered Harvard University as a member of the class of 1924. It was a notable one, including a future diplomat named Henry Cabot Lodge, a poet, Ogden Nash, and a book publisher, Frederick Roberts Rinehart.

In the spring of 1924, Jones was awarded an SB from Harvard. His major was English literature. His courses included English composition, comparative literature, Dryden and His Time, Swift and His Time, and Shakespeare. Jones also studied German prose, French, German, and English history, the history of the Roman Republic, and Continental Europe from 1815 to 1871. His foreign languages consisted of German and French. He was a member of the Owl Club and the Hasty Pudding Club.

Having already earned a degree, Jones was ineligible to play on the 1923 Harvard golf team. Desperately wanting to be any part of the team, he accepted the lowly position of assistant manager of the six-man squad, none of whom had ever qualified for a national championship. Six weeks after an informal match against Yale, Harvard's golf team's assistant manager was acclaimed as the greatest golfer in America. Many writers claimed him to be the best in the world.

On July 13, 14, and 15, the 1923 U.S. Open was played at the Inwood Country Club in Inwood, Long Island, a suburb twenty-three miles from New York City. The course was a long seaside layout—almost linkslike in quality—exposed to the swirling winds off the Atlantic Ocean less than a half mile away, and those of neighboring Jamaica Bay, through the marshlands of which several fairways meandered. It was such a severe test of golf that there were only two sub-par rounds. Jones had one of them.

Going into the final round, Jones led by three shots; he figured a three-over-par 75 would win the championship for him. He was right. He played the front nine in two over par; he then got two birdies, and with only three holes to play was even par. He could breeze in.

Then Jones did what would become so characteristic of him. He slipped into mental complacency. He hit his second shot out-of-bounds on the sixteenth for a bogey. He over-pitched the seventeenth green and failed to get down a 10-footer for his par.

The eighteenth is a severe finishing hole, a 425-yard par 4, usually played into a stiff breeze. The fairway is narrow and straight, thickly lined with pine and oak trees and patches of clumpy grass. In front of the green is a menacing blue lagoon.

In three rounds Jones had played the hole in only eleven strokes. Now a par or a bogey would close the door on all contenders. Jones's drive was perfect. Into the stiff breeze he elected to play a high spoon shot. He pulled it badly, twenty yards left of the green. He still could pitch over a small pot bunker for a par or at worst a bogey. He waited five agonizing minutes as the marshals cleared an alleyway. He then pitched the ball directly into the bunker. Out in one, then two putts, and he had a double bogey. Slowly he walked off the green, completely drained and completely disgusted with himself. When Keeler met him, he hesitantly said, "Bob, I think you're champion."

"I didn't finish like a champion," Jones snapped. "I finished like a yellow dog." He then went into his room at the club and brooded.

Only one player still on the course could catch Jones. That was Bobby Cruickshank. He came to the seventeenth tee knowing he had to play the final two holes in only seven strokes. He parred the seventeenth. After a perfect drive down the eighteenth fairway, he laced a magnificent 2-iron shot. The ball came in high right to left, hit eighteen feet from the pin, and rolled five feet right of it. He holed the putt. He had caught Jones.

If Fate ever wanted to bless anyone, it could hardly find a more deserving person than Bobby Cruickshank. He was twenty-nine and stood only five feet four inches tall. In 1921, almost penniless, he and his wife and two-year-old daughter immigrated to the United States from Scotland. Long before he had birdied the seventy-second hole, he had shown the stuff he was made of in life's most severe test. During World War I, he was in the thick of combat in the Battle of Somme; at Ypres, he had seen his younger brother blown up. Captured by the Germans, he had been assigned to the same prison camp as Tommy Armour's older brother, Sandy, who was suffering from a dire case of dysentery. Cruickshank denied himself half of what scanty rations he received and gave them to help young Armour back to health. With three other prisoners, Cruickshank escaped and rejoined his outfit. Bobby Cruickshank was a very good and brave man.

The play-off began at 2:00 P.M. When Keeler saw Jones on Sunday morning, July 15, he was horrified. The youngster's face was badly drawn, and his eyes were deeply set back in his forehead; they had the gaze of a chess player who had just lost a knight and had contemplated his next move for a long, long time. Jones was anxious to even the score, not with Cruickshank, but with himself. He feared one of the worst possible feelings: that he was gutless.

By 2:00 P.M. the skies were overcast and there was a mild breeze sweeping in off Jamaica Bay. Cruickshank was favored. The betting was 10 to 7 he would beat Jones. Before the match, Jones had decided two things: to try to play the course and not Cruickshank, and to play boldly. It was an intensely fought match, with the nerves of both players stretched further and further on the rack. The lead shifted back and forth. Only three holes were halved. By the fifth hole, Cruickshank, playing beautiful golf, was two under par and led Jones by two shots. Then, at the sixth and eighth the Scot failed to get down two par putts of under ten feet; the players were tied at even par at the ninth.

By the twelfth, Jones led by two shots, but with bogeys at the fourteenth and the fifteenth against Cruickshank's pars, the match was tied once more. With a par at the sixteenth to the Scot's bogey, Jones again led. He faltered with a bogey at the seventeenth, and Cruickshank responded with a gutsy par. So after eighty-nine holes of championship golf, the two golfers were even. Their nerves were so highly pitched that a mere snap of a twig would have sent them jumping ten feet in the air.

Now the mild breeze had turned into a wind, and the darkening sky promised rain. Heavy clouds were moving in quickly off Jamaica Bay.

Cruickshank drove first and tried to hit a low hook into the wind, but he pulled it badly and the ball ended up on a road behind a tree. Jones's drive was down the right side of the fairway. The ball bounded down the hard ground, and then took a horrible kick onto a sandy patch on the edge of the rough. It was a mean, tight lie; the ball would have to be nipped perfectly. Jones was 190 yards from the green.

Cruickshank could only play short of the lagoon. Now it was up to Jones; he, too, could play safely. If he went for the green and failed, it would certainly end his hopes of winning the Open. Without the briefest hesitation, Jones took his 1-iron, addressed the ball, and swung. High into the gathering storm clouds the ball flew, veering neither a yard left nor right. For a moment Jones owned the sky. Over the lagoon the ball came, then dropped softly on the green, curling up to within six feet of the pin. That was the championship. The best the brave and fighting Scot would manage was a 6 to Jones's 4.

The age of Bobby Jones had begun. . . .

10

For the first time in history, during that summer of 1930, the U.S. Open was being broadcast live over the Columbia Broadcasting System. Ted Husing, using a portable transmitter and microphone, was reporting from the seventeenth and eighteenth greens. For two full hours, he had a score of runners reporting to him on what was happening elsewhere on the course. Another runner, who was reporting to Grantland Rice, was almost as famous as Jones. He was Frank Craven, one of the most popular actors of the time. Like Douglas Fairbanks, he just loved watching Jones play. That afternoon, more than 15,000 spectators swarmed over the course.

And what a thrill Jones gave them. Just when it appeared he had burned himself out from his spectacular morning round, he flickered again and again with brilliance. It was a golfing exhibition of nerve and courage.

A par on the first hole, then a bogey and a double bogey, and it looked like Jones was throwing it away. Then he birdied the fourth. But then birdie putt after birdie putt refused to drop, and Jones posted a front nine of 38, five strokes worse than his morning round.

His face was a map of worry. He parred the first three holes on the back nine and appeared to be settling down. Before he played the thirteenth, he heard that Macdonald Smith, that forty-two-year-old hound dog who had given him such a terrible chase in the British Open, had played a brilliant front nine of 34. Seven shots had separated the two at the beginning of the final round. Now Smith had picked up four big shots. At the thirteenth, a long downhill par 3, Jones pulled his tee shot into the left-side green bunker. It took him two shots to get out, and two putts for a double bogey 5. Jones was giving away shots to par not one but two at a time. Only one shot now separated him from Smith.

Then came a stretch of golf, completely uncharacteristic of Jones, but characteristic of a champion. While Walter Hagen could play a poor shot and then blithely play the next one perfectly as though the first never happened, Jones, constitutionally, could not. A bad shot stayed with him like an ugly wart.

At the fourteenth, a 444-yard par 4, Jones struck a beautiful mid-mashie shot (3-iron) ten feet from the pin. He holed the putt. A birdie. He parred the fifteenth. At the sixteenth, he pitched to within four feet of the pin for another birdie—his third consecutive birdie on the hole. Now the championship was his, or was it?

On the seventeenth, he pushed his brassie tee shot so badly that the ball went sailing over the right-side green bunker and hit a tree. Where the ball went, nobody knew. Several hundred people claimed the ball ricocheted into the lake. For five minutes, 200 people searched for the ball in vain—a lost ball and a stroke penalty. Jones dropped a ball on the fairway, pitched to the green, and two-putted. This made his third double bogey of the round, and every one on a par 3. Jones had let the door to the championship open again. Macdonald Smith was playing wonderful par golf while Jones was busy proving that a golfer's most potent adversary is himself.

At the eighteenth, Jones completely misjudged his second shot, and the ball just reached the front edge of the green, forty feet from the pin. The butterflies in his stomach had turned to hornets. Jones studied the putt for an unusually long time; three-putting was as real as the blazing sun. The ball had to go up a gentle slope, then a steeper one to a plateau on which the hole was cut.

Jones gave the ball a firm tap; it rolled quickly up the gentle slope, slowly up the steeper one, and then six feet from the cup the ball broke just slightly left, falling into the cup for a birdie 3 and the championship. What a final round Jones had played: three double bogeys, four birdies, and eleven pars for a 75. His total of 287 was one shot off the Open record.

Ironically, the order of the first three finishers in the U.S. Open was the same as it had been in the British Open: Jones first, Macdonald Smith second, and Horton Smith third.

At the presentation ceremonies, Horton Smith summed up the frustration of the pros for whom it had become so vital to stop Jones. "We've all tried hard to corner the elusive Mr. Jones, but haven't succeeded. We certainly would like to beat him better than anything else in the world, but we haven't had any experience in doing it."

Jones's victory at Interlachen equaled two records. It's doubtful that either will ever be surpassed. In winning the 1930 U.S. Open, Jones captured his fourth Open title, tying the record set by Willie Anderson, a magnificent turn-of-the-century golfer. This record was tied again by the ineffable Ben Hogan, who won his last and fourth U.S. Open in 1953.

With four U.S. Opens, Jones increased his total of U.S. and British Open victories to seven, equaling the record of Harry Vardon, who won six British and one U.S. Open.

The more you examine the record books of golf, the larger the triumphs of Jones and Vardon loom with every passing year. They are the only golfers since 1860, when the first British Open was played, and 1895, when the U.S. Open was inaugurated, to win a combination of seven Opens. Only two golfers have won six: Walter Hagen, with four British Opens and two U.S. Opens, and Jack Nicklaus with three Opens apiece. In all, Jones played only in eleven U.S. Opens and four British Opens. His seven victories constitute a winning record of 47 percent, an impregnable statistic.

PART FOUR

The Amateur

11

On November 18, 1930, fifty-two days after Jones had won the U.S. Amateur—and captured the Grand Slam—he announced his retirement from competitive golf.

"The abdication of Emperor Jones," as the sportswriters called it, shocked the sporting world. Jones was still young, healthy, and vigorous. His powers of concentration were as strong as ever. He could still face a crucial sidehill putt with the curve of doom in it and hole it to win a championship. He could have gone on winning championships for the next ten years.

Jones was only twenty-eight at the time, but that was deceptive. For more than half his life, fifteen years, he had played competitive golf, and there are few games that so severely tax a man's physical and mental stamina as year-in-and-year-out competitive golf.

In all, Jones's decision was a most sagacious one. While his fans lamented the loss of Jones on the golfing scene, they saw, as with his game, that touch of genius in his decision. It is the wisest of athletes who has the foresight and emotional maturity to retire at the zenith of his career, who can hold temptation at bay and resist just one more championship, which invariably leads to another, and another, until the body is fighting against the laws of nature.

On November 18, *The New York Times* ran a rare and rather long editorial on Jones's retirement, titled "Jones Holes Out." The editorial concluded, "With dignity he quits the memorable scene upon which he nothing common did or mean."

Even the way Jones announced his retirement was characteristic of him. There was no great last hurrah, no elaborate press conference with stirring speeches. Simply, Jones wrote a carefully worded statement, as dry and unemotional as if he were a lawyer presenting a brief to a client, and submitted it to Herbert H. Ramsey, vice president of the USGA, who then released it to the press.

Since Jones was about to embark on several lucrative ventures, which then placed him in a limbo position of being neither an amateur nor a professional, he saved the USGA considerable embarrassment of settling the ticklish matter by stating that he was an ex-amateur who had decided not to play professional golf. He never had and he never would.

Unlike now, and until just after World War II, amateur golf was amateur golf. It wasn't a stepping-stone to the professional ranks. Financially, there was little incentive to turn pro. There was no professional tour in the present definition of the word. In the winter there was only a smattering of tournaments in Florida and California. Total prize money was $2,000, with a third going to the winner, and the remainder to the low top-nine pros. In the 1926 U.S. Open, the total prize money was

$2,146. The low professional received $1,000. Playing exhibitions was how the pros earned money, and no professional played more exhibitions than the showman of professional golf, Walter Hagen. It was not unusual for The Haig to play forty-five exhibitions a month.

Then there was the social stigma. Even into the late 1920s, there was a residue of American Victorianism toward professional athletes. It was believed corruption lurked everywhere. The true sportsman and gentleman was the amateur athlete. Emblematic of the professional golfer's social standing, until 1938 in the U.S. and British Opens, "Mr." only prefixed the amateur's name on the scoreboard.

For eight wonderful years, the likes of which will never be seen again in golf, the name of Mr. Robert T. Jones, Jr., was usually at the top of the scoreboard after a championship, for from 1923 to 1930, Jones never was without a national title. Twice prior to 1930 he was national champion of Great Britain and the United States. When he abdicated, he was the yardstick against whom all great golfers would be measured.

After Jones had captured the 1923 U.S. Open, after "seven lean years" of trying to win a national championship, it appeared to his devoted public that he now was almost unbeatable. Yet there remained a major flaw in Jones's game. He was still wrestling unsuccessfully with the strategy of match play.

Jones was favored to win the 1923 U.S. Amateur, but in the second round he was beaten 2 and 1 by the eventual winner, Max Marston, who threw a string of birdies at Jones. Afterward, a very dejected Jones told O. B. Keeler that he felt he never would win the Amateur. "Somebody always goes crazy against me," he said.

Grantland Rice theorized why Jones continued to lose in match play. It was Jones's copybook style, his exquisite timing that seemed to rub off on his opponents who, consequently, came up with their best golf against Jones. It was a sound theory, but only half true.

O. B. Keeler believed Jones was too courteous toward his opponents, that he never could bring to bear any measure of real hate, or regard an opponent as a true enemy. Psychologically, this was valid, since golf had always been one of Jones's great passageways toward friendship. The real fault was simpler, however: Jones hadn't yet learned to play against that imperturbable economist, Old Man Par.

By the summer of 1924, Jones began carefully analyzing the value of even par scores. With even par he figured he would have won at least one Amateur and two Opens. Jones was as methodical in golfing calculations as Bill Tilden was in analyzing tennis matches. In a three-set match, Tilden figured, if a player won the first set, 80 percent of the time he would win the match. Jones felt par would win 80 percent of the time.

The acid test came in the 1924 Amateur at the Merion Cricket Club in the last week in September. In the early matches Jones played against some good golfers who, indeed, threw more than their normal share of birdies at Jones's pars. But Jones held to his new faith in par and came through match after match safely. His narrowest margin of victory was 3 and 2. Jones reached the semi-finals.

In playing against par, Jones hadn't yet found a foolproof winning formula, but it was close enough, and as significant as if he had discovered the good seed.

Nobody had gone crazy against him. At least, not yet.

Jones's semi-finalist opponent was Francis Ouimet, that Bostonian who, at the age of nineteen, had dramatically beaten Harry Vardon and Ted Ray in a play-off to win the 1913 U.S. Open. It was Ouimet, one of the kindest men who ever played golf, who had spent tireless hours consoling Jones after he had blown up on the seventy-second hole of the 1923 Open. There was no one in competitive golf whom Jones liked better or for whom he had a greater respect. But now, on an emotional level, Jones couldn't regard even Ouimet as a friendly foe. Now his foe had to be par.

The result was the most lopsided match of the championship. Jones beat Ouimet 11 and 10. When the match ended on the twenty-sixth green, no one appeared less a victor than Jones. Rather, he looked like a man who had just been notified that his bank balance was overdrawn.

In the finals, Jones beat George Von Elm 9 and 8, the second-highest winning margin in the history of the U.S. Amateur.

By now the name of Bobby Jones was a household word. A sentimental, all-American touch was added to Jones's popularity when, on June 18, 1924, he married his high school sweetheart, Mary Rice Malone.

She was a pretty girl with handsome features—a classic oval face, long, thick, black-brown hair, usually worn parted down the middle, deep-set brown eyes, and an ivory-white skin with a flawless complexion. She was five feet six inches tall and had soft shapely legs and a full bosom. She kept herself meticulously well groomed and, in a sundress—usually her favorite color, red—she exuded a shy but very coquettish sensuality, more than enough to arouse the sexually innocent Bobby Jones.

Mary Malone was an uncomplicated girl raised with a feeling of entitlement. She grew up in Atlanta's exclusive Druid Hill section in a financially comfortable family. Her young years were marked by the influence of an overprotective father, and one older and one younger brother. Following her father's religion, to which her mother had converted, Mary was a devout Catholic. She never missed Mass either at Atlanta's Sacred Heart Church or later at Christ the King Cathedral.

Her father, John Malone, was a second-generation Irishman, a tax assessor for the city of Atlanta, and a landowner whose properties were inhabited by a segment of Atlanta's black population. Her mother, Mamie Rice Malone, came from an old, socially prominent family from Augusta; her father had served as a captain in the Civil War. While Mary inherited her father's quick Irish temper, from her mother she inherited a slightly husky Augusta accent and a definite social bearing.

With the mother's social connections, the Malones inched their way into Atlanta's society. When Mary Malone was eighteen, she made her debut at the Piedmont Driving Club and became a member of Atlanta's Junior League.

Being one of the few Catholic families in Atlanta society, Mary grew up with a keen social consciousness. She overcompensated for her unconscious fear of social rejection by becoming very exacting and prim in her behavior. To Mary, good manners marked the person. Orderliness was next to godliness.

The emotional attraction between Bob and Mary was one of opposites. Having only attended Atlanta's Mary Washington's Seminary for Girls, Mary was educated and raised to be an ideal lady of leisure. There was merely a modicum of intellectual compatability between the two.

Although she was married to America's greatest golfing genius, Mary never did try to comprehend the nature of golf, and only played because it was the social thing to do. At championships, she would get so nervous about Bob she never did follow him around; as was the more usual custom of the time, she sat with the other players' wives on a clubhouse veranda, usually wearing a large straw hat to protect her delicate skin.

While she enjoyed her husband's fame, she couldn't accept the price that went with it. Like many wives of famous men, she hated to share her husband with the world. Privately, she threw stormy fits of jealousy. That day in 1930 when Jones retired from competitive golf was one of the happiest days of their married life.

What she did give her husband was an almost selfless devotion, and a self that projected a need to which Jones could respond with an almost paternal protectivism. Mary was barely five months younger than Bob, but she guarded those months as if they were fifteen years. These were childish emotions she enjoyed, but then, Mary Malone Jones always remained the child of her own dreams.

12

In his bid for a second Open title, Jones was thwarted twice by two of the most unlikely golfers of the time.

In 1924, three months before Jones carried off his first Amateur, the Open was played at Oakland Hills Country Club in the Detroit suburb of Birmingham. Jones was tied for the lead at the halfway mark. On the final day the winds were blowing with such force that it seemed as if all the sand in the bunkers would end up in Detroit. Jones slipped to a final round 78, though with the dim satisfaction of holing a long putt on the final hole to secure second place.

The man to whom Jones stood second was a little Englishman named Cyril Walker, the pro at the Englewood Country Club in New Jersey. A month prior to the championship, Walker had had a strong hunch he was going to win the Open. At least so he told his wife, Elizabeth, whom he called "Tet," and she accompanied him to Oakland Hills to give moral support and make sure Cyril didn't stay up half the night drinking. In the howling winds of the final day, Walker, who had learned his golf on the windswept links of Hoylake, kept his ball low, beneath the wind, and finished with three beautiful pars. Although he never again came close to winning a national championship, that day he played like a champion, making a storybook tale come true.

In the 1925 Open, played at the Worcester Country Club in Worcester, Massachusetts, it was not the howling wind that got the golfers, but the heat. It was over 100 degrees in the shade. The sun didn't seem to shine so much as strike down on the players. Jones lost twelve pounds during the championship. He started with a 77 and followed with two 70s to play himself into contention.

That Open remains memorable for two things: the integrity of Bobby Jones shining as brilliantly as the sun, and one of the most exciting finishings of any Open.

In the first round, Jones played a poor iron shot left of the eleventh green; the ball ended up in some tall grass. As he addressed the ball, it moved ever so slightly. Even though no one but Jones had seen the ball move, he immediately penalized himself a stroke, and so informed the officials of the USGA. They felt that since he hadn't caused the ball to move he was being far too harsh on himself. Jones insisted unyieldingly, and the case was closed. Later, when someone told Jones what an honest thing he had done, he quietly snapped back in that soft southern accent, "You might as well praise a man for not robbing a bank."

At the time of the incident, O. B. Keeler had a queer hunch that the Open would be decided by a single stroke and that Jones would be involved. He was as right as Cyril Walker had been in his hunch a year before.

As the final round got under way, eight players had the

championship in their grasp if they could bring in a round of 70. Down the stretch they came, each very capable of doing it: Walter Hagen, Leo Diegel, Johnny Farrell, Jones, Francis Ouimet, Willie MacFarlane, Gene Sarazen, and Mike Brady. Unfortunately, no one brought in a 70. The best were four 74s. Jones had one, giving him a total of 291. It was one less shot than either Farrell or Ouimet, and two less than Sarazen or Hagen. Only Willie MacFarlane could catch Jones. On the eighteenth hole, a short 335-yard par 4 with a severely sloping raised green surrounded by a platoon of bunkers, MacFarlane hit his pitch to the rear of the green. He then just barely tapped his putt. The ball trickled slowly down the slope and stopped one foot from the cup, in a pitch mark. Feeling the mark might affect his putt, MacFarlane calmly took his 2-iron and chipped the ball into the cup, establishing a play-off with Jones.

Such antics were not unusual for MacFarlane. Basically a club pro from Oak Ridge Country Club in Tuckahoe, New York, MacFarlane could play his home course left-handed and shoot in the 90s, sometimes even in the 80s. Right-handed, he could be even more of a wizard, once playing ten consecutive rounds under 70.

A tall, thin, thirty-five-year-old Scottish-American, MacFarlane looked more like a high school principal than a golfer, and when he wore his rimless glasses, he looked like a poetry professor. He didn't particularly like the battle of tournament golf, entering only upon the urging of his friends, but he always enjoyed playing the Open, although unlike Cyril Walker he never had the dimmest dream he would win it. When the opportunity presented itself, however, he showed he had the game and guts.

The blistering heat continued on Sunday, June 5, as Jones

and MacFarlane squared off. At the fourteenth hole, it appeared MacFarlane had the championship. His second shot had stopped less than eight feet from the pin, and he led by a stroke. Jones's ball was sixty feet away off the green. He promptly chipped the ball in for a birdie. A startled MacFarlane missed his putt, but stayed in the fight. At the eighteenth, Jones had to work hard to get down a slippery 5-footer for a tie-matching par, but he made it.

In the afternoon, Jones broke quickly and after nine holes had built up a four-shot lead. MacFarlane slowly whittled away at it. At the par-3 tenth and thirteenth, he picked up two deuces against Jones's par and bogey. At the fifteenth, he picked up another birdie to Jones's par.

Going down the seventeenth fairway Jones said to Keeler, "This thing is getting funny. Still tied after one hundred and six holes." He did not add that he had played that amount in three days.

"Looks like a third play-off," Keeler said.

"There won't be another play-off. I'll settle it one way or another in this round."

The players tied the seventeenth. At the short eighteenth, MacFarlane put his pitch in the middle of the green. The pin was tucked twelve feet from the front bunker in a small hollow. Jones aimed to hit a foot over the bunker and let the ball roll to the pin. He missed by four inches. The ball hit the very top of the bunker and rolled back. A five to MacFarlane's four, making the final scores: Jones 75-73; MacFarlane: 75-72. For his efforts, MacFarlane won $500.

It had been a single-shot difference. Without the penalty shot Jones had imposed on himself, there would have been no play-off. While Keeler could rationalize for thousands of words about Jones, he rarely was closer to the truth than when he wrote, "There are things in golf finer than winning championships."

That September at the Oakmont Country Club, Jones won his second Amateur. His lowest winning margin was 6 and 5. The sensation of the championship wasn't Jones, however, but his protégé, a twenty-year-old youngster from Atlanta named Watts Gunn. Jones had coached and primed Gunn for competitive golf. In their regular matches around East Lake, Jones always gave Gunn three strokes a round.

A month before the championship, Jones had gone to see Watts's father, Judge Will Gunn, to plead with him to send Watts to the Amateur and give him tournament experience. Jones guaranteed he would look after Watts like a father.

In his first national championship, Gunn played inspiring golf. Over one stretch, he played fifty holes in even par. He gained his way to the finals against Jones. For the first and only time in the history of the U.S. Amateur, two men from the same club met in the finals. The question most commonly asked that day was "Why didn't they play this at East Lake and save carfare?"

On the first tee, Watts turned to Jones and said, "Bob, are you going to give me my three shots?"

"I'm going to give you hell today," Jones replied.

For the first eleven holes it was Gunn who was giving his master hell, playing under par and holding a 1-up lead. On the long par-5 twelfth, Gunn was safely on the green in three, and Jones had bunkered his third shot. As he climbed into the bunker, Jones recalled how it had been on the twelfth, a hole called the "Ghost Hole," that he had blown up in the 1919 Amateur. Now he harbored that queer premonition that if he lost the hole, he would lose the match. He gathered his wits and popped the ball out of the sand ten feet from the pin and

156

holed the putt. True, a halve was good for his game, but better still for Jones's sense of self-confidence. He played the next six holes, one of the most difficult stretches of holes in America, in 3-3-4-3-3-4, two under par, to go 4 up. He eventually won 8 and 7.

Returning to Atlanta, Jones confessed his ambition to Keeler. "O.B., if I could be a national champion of the United States, either Open or Amateur, for six years in succession, then I'd feel that I could hang up the old clubs." Although he was halfway there, neither he nor Keeler thought it was possible. They didn't speak about it again for years.

13

In 1926 the tennis court, the English Channel, the boxing ring, the baseball diamond, and the golf course were the testing grounds on which America's sporting heroes truly became the Golden People of the Golden Age of Sport. What a year it was for great sporting deeds. Athletes conquered the elements, challenging each other for supremacy, testing their own iron nerve. Hero worshiping was as much part of the American scene as the flapper, and there was a sporting hero for every American to worship.

In February 1926, America's favorite woman tennis player, Helen Wills, three-time winner of the Women's U.S. Singles at Forest Hills (she would win the Women's U.S. Singles seven times, Wimbledon Singles eight times, and the French Singles four times), went on the stalk for the only player said to be better than herself: Mlle Suzanne Lenglen, six-time Wimbledon Women's Singles champion. Days before the match was scheduled at the Carlton Tennis Club in Cannes, France,

Americans literally prayed for "Our Helen" to win; but, alas, the prayers seemed to go unanswered. In two thrilling sets, Mlle Lenglen beat Miss Wills 6–2 and 8–6. There was no triumphal return to the United States for Helen Wills, no heroine's welcome, and no ticker-tape parade.

Accolades went, however, to another very wholesome young American girl, Gertrude Ederle, just eighteen and the daughter of a delicatessen owner in New York City. On August 6, 1926, she became the first woman to swim the English Channel.

On September 24, 1926, at Sesquicentennial Stadium in Philadelphia in a torrid rainstorm, Jack Dempsey, the supposed invincible heavyweight champion, was dethroned by Gene Tunney. Regardless of having lost the title, it was still Dempsey, so savage in the ring and so vulnerable to tenderness and kindness out of it, who would remain the Golden fighter.

On April 9, 1926, Lou Gehrig started his first full season for the New York Yankees. There he would remain for an amazing 2,130 consecutive games.

Until 1930 Bobby Jones considered 1926 to be his best golfing year. It was bracketed by defeats, but in between Jones rose to ever-higher stardom.

The year began inauspiciously when, on Sunday, February 28, and the following Sunday, March 7, Jones played Walter Hagen in a seventy-two-hole match. After the time Jones had torn up his scorecard in the 1921 British Open, this match was his second most dismal moment in golf. While listed as a contest between "the amateur and professional champions," it was clearly a challenge match for top supremacy. Hagen had won the 1922 and 1924 British Opens, and the 1924 and 1925 PGA Championships. Jones took one of the worst beatings of his career, losing 12 and 11.

Walter Hagen's record in major championships is surpassed only by that of Bobby Jones and Jack Nicklaus. "The Haig" won eleven major championships, four in a row at match play from 1924 to 1927, winning an incredible twenty-two consecutive matches.

Hagen had the touch and nerve of a brain surgeon. He probably played more golf than any professional, yet never had a callus on his hands. While having smooth hands may appear to be an insignificant point, it is actually a very important one: his grip and pressure on the golf club were absolutely perfect.

His theatrical timing was also impeccable. He could make a simple bunker shot appear more dramatic than another player's hole-in-one. And if the golf course was Hagen's stage, nowhere did he perform better than on center stage: on the green. He was a great putter, but then he had to be. Of all the great golfers, there probably was none worse from the tee to green than Hagen; yet he had this uncanny ability to hit recovery shots that appeared impossible, and then hole a long putt for his par.

As the noted British golf writer, A. C. M. Croome, wrote of Hagen: "He makes more bad shots in a single season than Harry Vardon did from 1890 to 1914, but he beats more immaculate golfers because, 'three of those and one of them counts 4,' and he knows it."

From the time he broke into big-time golf at the age of twenty-two, when he won the 1914 U.S. Open, until the mid-1930s, when he was in his midforties, Walter Hagen had the same manner. He could be playing golf with the Prince of Wales or in a small Midwestern town, it didn't matter—his philosophy was the same, paraphrased as: "Never hurry and don't worry. You're here for just a short visit, so don't forget to stop and smell the flowers along the way."

Bobby Jones was at the other end of the personality spectrum. He was a terrible worrier. He feared looking foolish on the golf course; he feared the possibility of three-putting; he feared being beaten in match play by double figures; he feared not qualifying for a championship. All but the last came true in the 1926 match with Hagen.

Jones had taken on the task more out of a business interest than a golfing one. After he had graduated from Harvard he had gone to work as a real estate salesman for the prominent Atlanta firm of Adair Realty Company. Besides owning vast acreage in downtown Atlanta, Adair also held vast land holdings around Sarasota, Florida. Coincidentally, the first thirty-six holes of the Jones/Hagen match were played on the Whitfield Estates Country Club, contiguous to land owned by Adair Realty.

The other thirty-six holes were played over Hagen's nearby club, the Pasadena Golf Club. Hagen was playing well. After one three-under-par round of 69, it was reported that Hagen had gone around in sixty-nine strokes and Jones in sixty-nine cigarettes. Hagen took the total gate of $11,800. He gave $5,000 to the St. Petersburg Hospital, and then sent Jones a pair of 24-carat gold cuff links.

Walter Hagen was the first golfer to earn over $1 million playing golf and to spend $2 million. Although he did spend an excessive amount of money on cars, fancy clothes, women, and champagne, he also gave hundreds of thousands away to struggling golfers and charities. Hagen may have set a record in the PGA Championship that will never be surpassed, but he also set a record of having more fun with the money he spent than anyone else in golf.

By insisting on going first class, Hagen, or Sir Walter as he was sometimes called, helped to break down the class barrier between the amateur and professional golfer. "Golf never had a showman like him," Gene Sarazen once said. "All the professionals who have a chance to go after the big money today should say a silent thanks to Walter Hagen each time they stretch a check between their fingers. It was Walter who made pro golf what it is."

The lopsided defeat Jones received by Hagen sent Jones on a worrying binge. He had been outplayed, beaten in double figures. He had taken eleven more putts than Hagen. His iron play had been its worst in years.

With a full schedule coming up, Jones had to do something and do it fast. He put himself under the capable teaching of Tommy Armour, who already was gaining a reputation as a fine teacher. Armour and his assistant quickly diagnosed Jones's problem: he was using too much right hand on his iron shots. They emphasized a firmer left-hand control, and using the right only for continuing momentum through the shot. Within days, Jones again was drilling his irons straight on line. The lesson had come none too soon.

The British Amateur began on May 24, at Muirfield, The Honourable Company of Edinburgh Golfers, on the east coast of Scotland. Jones got through the fourth round easily, and then in the fifth he really came on top of his game, defeating the defending British Amateur, Robert Harris, 8 and 6. But again, like the sudden shifting of the wind, Jones was then beaten in the sixth round by a relatively unknown Scottish golfer, Andrew Jamieson, 3 and 2. It was the upset of the championship, with Jamieson as much surprised as anyone. He later wrote Jones a note in Latin apologizing for winning and calling himself "an imprudent fool." Such was Jones's hold on Britain's golfers.

Jess Sweetser, suffering so severely from a case of influenza that from time to time he had to be administered morphine by Keeler, ended up winning the British Amateur.

The next week, on June 2 and 3, the Walker Cup matches were played at St. Andrews. In those two days a love affair began between the citizens of St. Andrews and Bobby Jones that would span forty-five years.

As the U.S. Amateur champion, Jones was positioned in the number-one spot, and in the singles matches over thirty-six holes, he beat Cyril Tolley 12 and 11, somewhat redeeming his 12 and 11 loss to Hagen. The United States won 6 to 5. Ten hours after the competition, Jess Sweetser, that valiant warrior, fell desperately ill. He would spend a year recovering in Asheville, North Carolina.

With the rest of the U.S. Walker Cup team, Jones had booked his passage to New York on the *Aquitania*. He dearly missed Mary, now five months pregnant, and his daughter, Clara, now two years old. But two days before he was to sail, Jones cancelled his reservation. He had decided to play in the British Open: Jones, who prided himself on his sportsmanship, still felt rankled over his childish conduct in the 1921 British Open, and felt further that his British admirers hadn't yet seen his best golf. Jones was out to make amends. What happened in the next two weeks had British hearts throbbing.

Jones led the qualifying for the British Open by seven shots. He shot a 66 and a 68 over the Sunningdale golf course. In thirty-six holes, except for three pitch shots, he only used a short iron once and his mashie iron (4-iron) twice. All the rest of his shots to the green were either with long irons or woods.

While a 66 is always a good score, the way Jones composed it makes it sing even today, more than a half-century later, as one of the finest rounds of golf ever played. Except for the par-3 thirteenth, where Jones bunkered his tee shot, then

163

pitched out and holed his putt for a par, he hit every green in regulation figures. He was on the green of the four par 5s in two, hitting two greens with brassie shots, one green with a 1-iron, and another with a mid-iron. Thus on thirteen holes he was putting for birdies, and on four holes he was putting for eagles. He hit exactly 33 shots, stroked 33 putts, went out in 33, and came in in 33. There was neither a 5 nor a 2 on his card, only 3s and 4s. "I love a round with only 4s and 3s on it," Jones wrote later. "The implication of such a round is that you are shooting golf and not carrying horseshoes."

With the completion of the round, Bernard Darwin wrote, "After that the crowd dispersed awe-stricken. They had watched the best round they had ever seen or ever would see, and what the later players did they neither knew nor cared."

Here was a very happy Jones, but also a very worried Jones. He felt that his game had peaked too soon, six days before The Open, and that he couldn't keep the streak going.

The Open was played at Royal Lytham and St. Annes, outside Southport, England, on June 23, 24, and 25. In winning, Jones displayed four rounds that epitomized what the great English golfer, John H. Taylor, called "courageous timidity."

If Jones's putting was on, his drives or iron play were off. To fashion a first round of even par 72, he had to one-putt the last four greens. After another par round, he led by two shots.

Two shots back was Al Watrous, a fine, big blond American pro from Grand Rapids. In the third round, Watrous fired a 69 to Jones's 73; he led by two. They were paired together for the final round.

After the third round, Watrous, Jones, and Keeler had gone to Jones's room in a nearby hotel to relax and have some ham sandwiches and tea. When they returned to the course, Jones discovered he had forgotten his player's badge, and the attendant, not knowing who Jones was, wouldn't allow him in. Without the slightest fuss, Jones went to the spectators' entrance, paid five shillings, and entered; thus Bobby Jones became the only player in British Open history to pay to watch himself win.

In the final round, the power and accuracy returned to Jones's drives, but his putting soured. He took a total of thirty-nine putts, not one-putting a single green. Through the tenth hole, he three-putted three times, and still trailed Watrous by two shots. But three-putting can be as contagious as the common cold, and Watrous three-putted the fourteenth and fifteenth. Both players parred the sixteenth. The Open had narrowed down to these two men, with two holes to play.

At the seventeenth, a par 4 of 411 yards, slight dogleg left, Watrous struck a beautiful drive and followed it with a mashie to the right edge of the green. Advantage Watrous. Jones hooked his drive, and the ball settled in a fairway bunker 175 yards from the green. Worse, he had a blind shot, into a slight breeze, over a large sand dune to the green. If he wanted to win, it was the only shot he had.

Jones desperately needed a par 4. He could have studied the shot longer than he did, but he simply took his mashie iron (4-iron), walked into the bunker, took his stance, looked once at the line, and swung with that seemingly effortless pivot. He nipped the ball off the sand perfectly, spraying no more than a powder puff of sand. The ball climbed quickly and straight, was held up slightly by the mild wind, and came down on the green with so very little overspin . . . Jones's ball rolled closer to the pin than Watrous's ball.

It was a courageous shot; Jones had literally thrown timidity to the wind. Unnerved, Watrous three-putted for a bogey to Jones's par, and when the American pro drove into a fairway bunker on the eighteenth, that was it. Jones won by two shots. In the clubhouse he was congratulated by more than forty former British Amateur and Open champions, who unanimously agreed the best player had won The Open. To this day, Jones remains the only American to win the British Open at Royal Lytham and St. Annes.

A very happy Bobby Jones sailed for New York. There he was met by Mary and his family, including Robert Tyre Jones, Sr., who claimed all the while he was really in New York on business, rather than to celebrate. There was a ticker-tape parade up Broadway in which Jones was chaperoned by Jimmy Walker and Major John Cohen, publisher of the *Atlanta Journal.* For Bobby Jones and the citizens of Atlanta, all was well with the world.

Two weeks later Jones was going after his second national title, playing in the U.S. Open at the Scioto Country Club in Columbus, Ohio. A bloodhound with the scent couldn't have been more determined than Jones.

He started off smartly with a two-under-par 70, and no one could assess, from even the blink of an eyelid, that two months of competitive golf had produced the slightest strain on Jones. Jones was the golfing machine, reporters were writing.

The next day Jones went out and proved how very human he was by shooting a horrid 79, ending with a double bogey 7 on the 480-yard, par-5 eighteenth.

On the morning of the final day of play of thirty-six holes, Jones felt so nauseous he had to see a doctor, who gave him something to calm his stomach. Jones then went out and shot a respectable 71, putting him three shots behind the leader, Joe Turnesa.

Jones had a light lunch of tea and a toasted chicken sandwich, but he couldn't keep even that down. Feeling almost as sick as he had in the morning, he started his final round. The chase was on, with the odds against Jones catching Turnesa before the nervous strain fully caught him.

Jones bogeyed the par-3 ninth for the fourth time. He stood on the tenth tee exhausted, every muscle tired, every nerve strained, and four shots behind Turnesa, who was playing two pairs in front of him. Jones now was facing the most difficult test of golf in the United States, the final nine holes of the U.S. Open.

Jones equaled Turnesa's pars at the tenth and eleventh. At the long 545-yard, par-5 twelfth, Turnesa, playing boldly, went for the green in two; but his second shot caught a bulge of rough near the green. A bogey 6. Jones also went for the green in two and hit a long, low brassie shot that just made the fringe. He chipped eight feet past the cup, then holed the putt. A birdie 4.

Turnesa took another bogey on the long par-4 thirteenth, which was playing into a quartering wind, demanding a spoon or brassie to reach the green. Jones hit a high spoon shot just left of the green, hoping the wind would drift the ball right. It didn't, and the ball landed in the far side of a shallow bunker left of the green.

The ball couldn't have been in a worse position. The hole was cut no more than twelve feet from the bunker's edge on a terrace, beyond which the green sloped severely downhill. Even the most delicate explosion shot would come out without backspin and roll down the hill past the hole. What Jones did was another touch of genius. He took his mashie and ran the ball through the sand; it rolled up the bank with just the right speed, onto the green, and stopped four feet from the hole. He holed the putt for a par. Now he was only one shot back with five holes to play.

He followed Turnesa's pars at the fourteenth and fifteenth. At the sixteenth, Jones finally caught him with a par against a bogey. Jones went ahead at the par-3 seventeenth, when Turnesa made his only major mistake of the day and hit his iron short of the green, then failed to get down a par putt. Jones parred it.

But Turnesa wasn't quitting. He made a wonderful birdie 4 at the eighteenth, forcing Jones to go for the green in two. Smelling victory, Jones smashed one of his longest drives of the championship—over 300 yards and straight down the middle of the fairway, now lined with more than 10,000 spectators. Then, without the slightest sign of hurry or worry, Jones addressed his iron shot. He hit a beauty. Before the ball was halfway to the green, the cheers rolled down through the open valley. The ball hit the front edge of the green, almost struck the pin on the second bounce, and rolled sixteen feet past.

Then Jones hit a very careful first putt that stopped less than four inches from the cup. As he stepped up to tap in the winning putt, he suddenly was seized with a weird thought, "What if I should stub my putter into the turf and fail to move the ball?" Jones carefully addressed the tiny putt with the putter blade an inch off the turf and half-topped the ball into the cup. The frantic chase was over. How magnificently Jones had played. After the sixth hole, he had scored ten 4s and two 3s. But what an emotionally Pyrrhic victory it was.

In the players' locker room, Walter Hagen was fuming. He unleashed an angry lecture to his fellow pros. "Whenever I fail to stop Jones," said Hagen, who had finished sixth, "the rest of you curl up and die, too. All the God damn amateur has to do is show on the first tee, and the best pros in the world throw in the towel. What are we going to do about it?"

In his hotel room in Columbus, Jones sat sipping a highball.

He had not even finished a quarter of it when, without any provocation, he burst into a fit of tears. They rolled over his sunburned face in a stream. His strong muscular body trembled like jelly. Not one spectator at Scioto would have guessed that the man they saw—who exhibited what Ernest Hemingway would describe as style "of grace under pressure"—internally was so very high-strung. There was no outward sign when he played that before each shot he had to consciously quiet his nerves . . . or that later, with the combat over, he would end up crying in a hotel room in Columbus.

After the Open, the Amateur championship—being played at the historic Baltusrol Golf Club in Springfield, New Jersey—should have been a runaway for Jones. At least, so it appeared. Jones was medalist for the third time in the Amateur, and he was nine shots lower than his nearest rival. But in the very first match, at eighteen holes, Jones just barely won. After birdieing the thirteenth, he held on tenaciously to a 1-up lead. From then on Jones's slimmest margin of victory was 3 and 2. In the finals, he again met George Von Elm from Rancho, California. Von Elm, who had almost failed to qualify, knew that to beat Jones he had to beat par; he did just that. When Jones failed to get down a 7-foot birdie putt at the thirty-fifth hole, the match was over. For the first time in the history of the U.S. Amateur, the trophy was taken to California. That was the last time Jones was beaten over thirty-six holes at match play.

When Jones returned to Atlanta, he didn't go back to the Adair Realty Company. Two years of selling real estate had been more than enough for him, particularly since selling seemed alien to his nature. With his strong sense of fair play, his lack of shrewdness, utter incomprehension of bargaining, and his introverted and shy personality, Bobby Jones was a misfit as a salesman.

He was also beginning to consider himself a misfit as a celebrity. More and more he treasured his privacy, and wondered if competitive golf was a game worth the candle. He was twenty-four at the time.

Law was the best option open to him, and he entered Emory University Law School.

In his first year, Jones took Public Utilities, Agency, Contracts, Damages Pleading and Practice, Property, and Torts. He withdrew from Emory in the fall of 1927 to take his bar exam. In 1928 he was admitted to the Georiga Bar and joined his father's law firm of Jones, Evins, Moore and Powers.

Because of his studies and lack of finances, Jones didn't compete in the 1927 British Amateur; but in the early spring, he did play—for the final time—in the Southern Open at East Lake. He won by eight shots over Johnny Farrell. As yet, the pros were not stopping Jones.

They finally did at the 1927 Open at the Oakmont Country Club. Jones was driving poorly, trying to avoid the bunkers, and not even Calamity Jane could redeem the situation. Jones had his poorest Open. He started with a 76 and followed with a 77. He finished tied for eleventh place.

The Open was won by Tommy Armour. He came to the seventy-second hole needing a birdie to tie Harry Cooper. Armour struck his iron shot eight feet from the pin. Then, with all the fighting instincts of a man who, in World War I, lost an eye, caught eight pieces of shrapnel in his left shoulder, and jumped out of the turret of his tank to break the neck of a German officer with his huge, strong hands, he calmly sank the putt. He beat Cooper by three shots in the play-off.

The pros had only stopped Jones temporarily. He returned to Atlanta, where Maiden straightened out his driving, then

170

24. Prior to the first round of the 1930 U.S. Open, Jones and his playing companion, Jock Hutchison. So hot and humid was the day that Jones's red florid tie ran over his shirt.

25. Jones holes a 40-foot birdie putt on the eighteenth green in the final round to clinch the 1930 U.S. Open. What a round it was: twelve pars, three double bogeys, and three birdies.

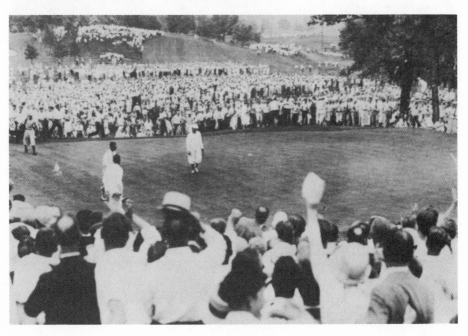

26. During a practice round of the 1930 U.S. Amateur: O. B. Keeler, who covered all thirty-one of Jones's national championships, strides to the next tee with Jones and Chuck Ridley, Jones's informal bodyguard.

27. September 24, 1930—Jones drives off the first tee at the Merion Cricket Club near Philadelphia in the first round of the U.S. Amateur, the last championship Jones had to annex to capture the Grand Slam.

28. Jones holes a 25-foot birdie putt on Merion's par-3 ninth. It was his third consecutive birdie as he beat his first-round opponent, Ross Somerville, 5 and 4.

29. Truly the last competitive shot Jones hit, a pitch to Merion's eleventh green in the finals of the 1930 U.S. Amateur.

30. End of the quest. Jones beats Eugene Homans 8 and 7 to win the 1930 U.S. Amateur and complete the Grand Slam. As his friend and faithful scribe O. B. Keeler wrote, "Others may attack in vain forever."

31. Jones poses with the Grand Slam trophies. Left to right: the British Open, U.S. Amateur, British Amateur, and U.S. Open.

went to Scotland to defend his British Open title and fulfill one of his lifetime dreams, to win a championship at St. Andrews.

Jones won the 1927 British Open in the finest Open championship of his career. Not once did he become complacent. He opened with a 68, tying the course record and followed with rounds of 72-73-72. He was never over par, and he broke The Open record by five shots, winning by six.

In the opening round, Jones thrilled the gallery of over 8,000 with his long, straight driving and his putting. He had only twenty-nine putts, not a remarkable total, but he didn't miss one under twelve feet. On six greens he was more than 100 feet from the pin, and five times got down in two putts. On the 533-yard, par-5 fifth, he reached the green in two and holed his long putt for an eagle. Later the putt was paced off at being more than 120 feet.

Less than five seconds after Jones holed his final winning putt, 12,000 Scots converged on Jones. Keeler, who was near the green, kept shouting in fear, "My God, they're going to kill him. They're going to kill him." Jones was lost in the sea of spectators. Then suddenly he appeared on top of the shoulders of a spectator, holding Calamity Jane high in the air, and was triumphantly marched to the Royal and Ancient Clubhouse.

As men often dream of the perfect woman, the Scots had long dreamed of what the perfect golfer would be. To them, Bobby Jones was that dream figure come to life.

In his usual brief and modest acceptance speech, Jones forever endeared himself to the hearts of the Scots. When presented with the trophy, he said, "Nothing would make me happier than to take home your trophy. But I cannot. It was played for here thirty years before I was born. Please honor me by allowing it to be kept here at the Royal and Ancient Club, where it belongs."

Jones carried his excellent golf into the 1927 U.S. Amateur at the Minikahda Club in Minneapolis the last week in August. Again he was medalist. He breezed easily to the finals and beat Chick Evans 8 and 7.

Combining his score in the British Open and the U.S. Amateur, Jones played a total of 224 holes of championship golf, or the equivalent of just over twelve rounds, in seventeen under par.

In June 1927, the New York publishing firm of Minton Balch & Company published Jones's autobiography, *Down the Fairway*, which Jones wrote with O. B. Keeler, with a foreword by Grantland Rice. The book had been serialized in *Liberty* magazine. By August it had gone into its third printing, and in all would go into five.

At that time amateur golfers could write golf instruction without jeopardizing their amateur status. (The USGA would change the rule in 1947.) In late summer 1927, Jones also began writing a column twice weekly for Bell Syndicate, which he continued to do until 1935. These columns, combined with all his other writings on golf, measured more than half a million words. Unlike other sporting heroes of the time who wrote "how to" columns with a ghostwriter, Jones alone was responsible for each of his. They varied in length from 150 to 300 words, and were perfectly structured, lucid, informative, never containing one meaningless word. While his columns appeared to be as effortless as one of his swings, Jones labored over each word. He hated any form of ambiguity. It was as if he had memorized every page of William Strunk's and

E. B. White's popular guide to lucid writing, *The Elements of Style.*

(It wouldn't have surprised anyone close to him if he had. In the early 1960s, when his granddaughter, Mary Jones, currently a fiction editor on a widely read magazine, misused a word in her grandfather's presence, he politely corrected her, and after she left, he promptly sent her a copy of *The Elements of Style.*)

In many of Jones's columns there appeared more golfing wisdom than might be found in a dozen golf instruction books.

On learning, he wrote: "Golf is the one game I know which becomes more and more difficult the longer one plays it."

On timing: "Nobody ever swung the golf club too slowly."

On shanking: "Although shanking is not the most universal of golfing mistakes, it certainly has the most demoralizing effect upon those who may be addicted to it; and once victimized, it seems that the greater the determination with which one tries to avoid it, the more will one foster the habit. Because the fear of shanking, by contracting the swing, induces shanking, the evil is cumulative, living upon itself . . . Shanking is a thing to cure, but not something to think about preventing."

On championship pressure: "One always feels that one is running from something without knowing exactly what or where it is."

14

By 1928 Jones truly began to suffer. Golf ceased to be the joyous game it had been. While his name had almost become synonymous with golf in America and Great Britain, and practically a suffix to Georgia's city of Atlanta, he was experiencing a certain dehumanizing aspect of the game. In the last two years, he had played in seven major championships and won four. Naturally, the more he won the more he was expected to win. The public and press were more astonished when he lost than when he won.

Jones's friends had begun gambling large sums of money on him to win, almost as if he were a racehorse. He soon discovered that when he lost, so did his friends. Just how much his friends might lose was an added burden he had to carry into competition. No wonder he began to feel more and more alone on the fairways.

There was pressure from the sportswriters who now criticized his abbreviated tournament schedule. But Jones remained emphatic that too many tournaments left him emotionally stale for the major championships. Also, his new law practice and young family were taking up a large portion of his time. He decided not to defend his British Open title, but concentrate his efforts on the U.S. Open and Amateur championships.

The 1928 Open was played at America's largest country club, Olympia Fields, outside Chicago, in the third week in June.

When it was over, Jones's eyes looked no larger than pinpoints, and he was near the brink of physical and emotional exhaustion. He had demonstrated again that the hardest thing in golf is to protect a lead in the Open, and that bad habits as well as good ones die hard. Again he had become beguiled by his own excellence.

Going into the final round, Jones led Hagen by three shots and Johnny Farrell by five. Hagen faded quickly. Jones played even par golf through the fourth and then, at the fifth, he holed a 10-foot birdie putt. He had a five-shot lead with thirteen holes to go. He next took a double bogey, a bogey, and two more bogeys. He finished the front nine in forty and, fighting off panic, came in in 37 for a 77 and a seventy-two-hole total of 294 to tie Johnny Farrell.

In the thirty-six-hole play-off, Farrell played dazzling golf, finishing the morning with three birdies and leading Jones by three shots. In the afternoon round, Jones, who hadn't been driving well, got back his drives and caught Farrell. By the twelfth, Jones led by one shot. At the par-3 thirteenth, Farrell holed a long putt for a 2, and the match was even. Jones bogeyed the sixteenth, his seventieth hole in two days, and was a shot behind with two to play. At the seventeenth, Farrell put his second shot less than four feet from the pin; Jones was thirty feet away. He holed his putt for a birdie. Farrell's putt now looked like thirty yards, but he holed it. Jones birdied the last hole, and Farrell holed his 10-footer for a birdie. Farrell had won by one shot.

The pros had stopped Jones for the second straight year. It was beginning to look like a permanent thing, but they were having their problems with reality and illusion. Except for 1927, from the time Jones won his first Open in 1923, he had either finished first or second; and until Jones retired, neither Walter Hagen nor Gene Sarazen led a single round in the Open.

Two months later, Jones was back in the Chicago area as captain of the Walker Cup team, with the matches to be played over the Chicago Golf Club, August 30 and 31. As U.S. Amateur champion, Jones placed himself in the number-one position.

Preparing for the matches, Jones played ten rounds. He broke two course records and tied one. He scored two 67s, four 68s, two 69s, one 70, and one 71, for an average of 68.5 strokes a round. In one round, for the Warren K. Wood Memorial Cup, Jones scored seven consecutive 3s for an incoming nine of 30.

In the Walker Cup matches, the United States won 11 to 1. In the singles competition, Jones beat the British Amateur champion, Thomas Perkins, 13 and 12.

Ten days later, the U.S. Amateur got under way at the Brae Burn Country Club outside Boston. Again, as in 1926, Jones was having trouble in the eighteen-hole matches. In the second round, he had to sink a slippery 17-foot putt on the sixteenth hole to stay in the match against an unknown named Robert Gorton. It went to extra holes with Jones winning 1 up. Once into the thirty-six-hole matches, Jones never played more than twenty-seven holes. His margins of victory were 14 and 13 in the quarter-finals, and 13 and 12 in the semi-finals. In the finals he met Thomas Perkins. The Englishman was anxious to even the score after his terrible beating by Jones in the Walker Cup, but Perkins didn't stand a chance. Jones won 10 and 9.

Bobby Jones had now been a national champion—winner of either the Amateur or the Open—for six consecutive years.

Shock and horror greeted the golfing fans in 1929 who came in the tens of thousands to watch Jones. What he did was almost lose one national championship, then hit one of the best shots ever struck in golf to redeem himself. Several months later he unexpectedly, and very promptly, lost another national title.

As in 1928, Jones concentrated his efforts on the two national championships of the United States. In the last week of June the U.S. Open was played over the West Course at Winged Foot Golf Club in Mamaroneck, New York, a suburb twenty-five miles north of New York City.

Jones arrived at Winged Foot ten days before the championship to work on his game. From the previous September to late April, he had played less than a dozen rounds of golf. His iron play had soured. For eight straight days he played Winged Foot, a long course with smallish greens, with narrow openings and steep-walled bunkers. If he didn't push his irons, he pulled them. Finally, on Tuesday, June 25, he began hitting his irons high and straight. As was his habit, he took off Wednesday, the day before the tournament.

He opened with a 69, and ended up the only player to break 70 during the championship. He followed with rounds of 75 and 71, and again led going into the final round; this time his lead was four shots.

By the time he reached the eighth hole, he had raced far ahead of the field, all of whom were having trouble in the high winds, deep bunkers, and slick greens. Jones had only to finish the front nine with two 4s for a 35 for an almost insurmountable lead. For the 10,000 spectators who had come to see the supposedly flawless golfer, what happened next caused literal gasps of horror.

Jones hit what looked like a lovely low punch shot into the wind to the eighth green. The ball hit just short of the green and bounded into the left-side bunker. From there, Jones blasted across the green into another bunker, and from there blasted again into the first bunker. He finally took a triple bogey 7. Now very bunker-shy, Jones began to play rather timidly. He got his pars, but couldn't get a birdie.

Playing ahead of Jones was Al Espinosa, a slow-moving Spanish-American from Monterey, California. When he reached the long par-5 twelfth, he was four shots behind Jones. He took a triple bogey 8. Thinking he had played himself completely out of contention, Espinosa just played in as a matter of routine. But how he played was hardly routine. With the pressure off, he came down the stretch in only twenty-two shots, with four 4s and two 3s. He was more surprised than anyone when he discovered he had shot a 75 for a total of 294, and led the field. Still, he figured he had no chance of winning; Jones was five shots ahead, and now playing consistent par golf.

At the thirteenth, Jones lost a shot to par. At the fifteenth, he badly sliced his drive, slashed his ball onto the fairway, then hit his pitch over the green. He then flubbed a delicate pitch. Finally on the green in five, he took his second triple bogey. Now he needed to finish with three 4s, over a stretch of holes that averaged just over 441 yards, to win by a shot.

At the sixteenth, he faced a 20-foot putt for a birdie. He left it four feet short, and then missed his par putt. He now needed two 4s to tie. He got his par at the seventeenth. His second shot to the eighteenth seemed fine but with a shade too much draw to it. The ball landed on the left edge of the green but didn't hold; it rolled into the bunker, stopping in some clumping grass. From there, Jones had to get down in two shots to tie. His pitch was weak.

What he faced to tie was a menacing 12-foot sidehill, downhill putt on a green as slick as glass. Borrowing more than a foot and a half on the slope, Jones barely tapped the ball. It rolled slowly, took the break, and then momentarily stopped on the lip of the cup, as if waiting for an angel's kiss, and dropped.

Jones hadn't won the Open, just a reprieve. The next day the play-off would start at 10:00 A.M., but Jones requested of the USGA that it be postponed an hour. He thought Espinosa might want to go to Mass. The request was granted. In the thirty-six-hole play-off, Jones beat Espinosa by twenty-three shots.

Grantland Rice claimed Jones's 12-foot par putt on the eighteenth green at Winged Foot was the greatest putt ever holed. He was convinced that if Jones had missed it, it would have shaken his confidence to the point where he probably never would have attempted the Grand Slam. There was more of the bone than the tissue of truth to his comment.

So treacherous was the putt that twenty-five years later, at a special celebration of the Grand Slam at Winged Foot, four pros—Tommy Armour, Johnny Farrell, Gene Sarazen, and Craig Wood—were given a chance to make the identical putt. None made it.

Early in September 1929, the U.S. Amateur was played for

the first time on the West Coast. It couldn't have been played at a better course: Pebble Beach Golf Links, then only ten years old and the least well-known of any great course in the country.

Jones was co-medalist with Eugene Homans at one over par. One hundred and sixty-two golfers tried to qualify for the thirty-two spots. One who failed to make it was a tool-die manufacturer named Howard Hughes.

The night before the first round, there was the usual heavy betting—this time in the form of a Calcutta pool, in which players are auctioned off to the highest bidder. If the bidder's man wins, he collects 75 percent of the pot, often in excess of $100,000. A Boston millionaire, Henry Lapham, invested $56,650, of which he paid $23,000 for Jones, $8,000 for Oui-met, and the remainder for several other players.

It was the highest anyone had ever paid for Jones in a Cal-cutta. No wonder he was more than usually nervous before his match with an unknown player from Omaha, Nebraska, Johnny Goodman, a man so poor he had traveled out to Cal-ifornia in a cattle car.

As O. B. Keeler would write, "Golf championships are a good deal like omelets. You cannot have an omelet without breaking eggs, and you cannot have a golf championship with-out wrecking hopes." Goodman beat Jones 1 up.

The golfing world was shocked. Only months later did Jones see his defeat as a blessing in disguise. As he told Keeler, he never learned anything from a match he won. Jones had always feared eighteen-hole matches, feeling that the run was too short. Once the fear had become a stark reality, he could hon-estly deal with it—not the easiest thing in golf, or in life. From then on in eighteen-hole matches, Jones realized he had to start fast. That's exactly how he intended to start every match in the 1930 British Amateur.

Instead of leaving Pebble Beach in a huff of anger, like a spoiled prima donna, Jones stayed around; he even refereed the third round, one of the most exciting of the championship, between George Voigt and Harrison Johnston. It went three extra holes, with Johnston winning 1 up and eventually winning the 1929 Amateur.

Jones also got to play Cypress Point, designed by Alister MacKenzie, whom he would later hire as codesigner of Augusta National.

While Jones was rightly disappointed over his defeat, Keeler was probably more deflated. With his man out of the hunt so early, he had little else to write about really, except the scenery. If Jones was impressed by Cypress Point, so was Keeler, who described it perhaps better than anyone else ever has. "Cypress Point is a dream—spectacular, perfectly designed, and set about white sand dunes, and a cobalt sea, and studded with the Monterey Cypress, so bewilderingly picturesque that it seems to have been the crystallization of the dream of an artist who has been drinking gin and sobering up on absinthe."

PART FIVE

The Second Journey

15

Jones harbored only one regret when he retired in 1930. He felt he hadn't reached the status of being a complete golfer. Preposterous? How could a man win thirteen major championships in eight years, including the Grand Slam, set records that have stood for more than half a century, and will probably stand forever, and call himself less than a complete golfer?

Only Bobby Jones, the rarest person to play golf, would set such standards. To him a complete golfer was one who had the ability to hold a lead and, with authority, wrap up a championship. While Jones holds the record of winning more Anglo-American national championships than any other golfer, he also holds several rather dubious U.S. Open records. With only eighteen holes to play, Jones led the Open six times; he won only three of those times. He was in a total of four play-offs, winning twice, and played a record of seven play-off rounds.

Of his inability to hold a lead, Jones incisively wrote, "Having reached the state where I suddenly knew that I should certainly win with any sort of ordinary finish, I became fearful of making myself look ridiculous by kicking the thing away. At this point, I think I began to be conscious of my swing and began to try to make too certain of avoiding a disastrous mistake. I was no longer playing the shots for definite objectives, but was rather trying to keep away from hazardous places."

To say that Jones retired because as a golfer he had conquered all the worlds there were to conquer is telling only the beginning of a story.

Jones's personal reasons for retiring pulled at him as strongly as the financial reasons. By 1930 Jones was golf—or as many people believed, golf was Jones. The affection the sporting world had for him was deep and loyal. Without the hoopla, only the feeling the sporting world has had for Arnold Palmer could come close to equaling its devotion to Jones.

While there is pressure enough being the best at what you do, there is a further and, perhaps, greater pressure trying to stay at the top. To be the most loved sportsman of your time is but another strain to carry into battle. You feel you can't let your subjects down. Jones was like the beloved monarch who could do no wrong on or off the course. So when he decided to bow from the scene, it was as a champion who would continue to live on as a champion.

Although he was never a loner, the severe loneliness that is part of championship golf had gotten to Jones. Hagen played to the galleries and loved the applause; Jones did not. He was always polite and courteous, and he acknowledged the affection and esteem of his fans, but that was the extent of it. He didn't need the applause. To him, the game was the thing. But by 1930, golf held little joy for Jones. Now he was anxious to rediscover the joy of a game that had become joyless for him.

Contrary to popular belief, Jones wasn't an independently wealthy man. With the help of his family, he did manage, just barely, to take care of his wife and daughter in the mid-1920s. By that time his father and mother had moved to a large white clapboard house on Lullwater Road, in the Druid Hill section of Atlanta. The house was staffed by four servants: chauffeur, cook, maid, and gardener. Bob and Mary lived there for three years.

It was one of those wonderful blessings that Mary and Clara Jones got along so well. Always very open and definite about her likes and dislikes, Clara made known her feelings for Mary. She adored her. Mary was to Clara the daughter she never had, and Clara introduced Mary as her daughter rather than her daughter-in-law. It was always that way, even after she and Bob left the big house.

In 1927 the members of the Atlanta Athletic Club raised $50,000 and gave it to Jones for a house he wanted on Northside Drive in the Northeast section of Atlanta. Jones accepted the gift, but then contacted the USGA to see if it would jeopardize his amateur status. It would. Immediately he returned the money. But Robert Tyre Jones, Sr., who knew the value and interest of a dollar, suddenly interceded. He lent his grandson exactly $50,000 under the terms that he repay him $1 a year.

In February 1928, the Joneses moved into the house, just three months after their son, named Bob Jones III, was born. Now with his law practice and writings, Jones was becoming more financially independent.

For four years entrepreneurs and promoters had been most conscious of Jones's grip on the golfing and non-golfing public. He had received numerous offers. One was to play the movie lead of the successful Broadway play *Follow Through* about a golf and tennis player who plays and sings himself to the top. It had run for two very successful years on Broadway. Jones wasn't interested.

While he played competitive golf, he played as an amateur, but once he chose to retire, it was like opening the floodgates. Offers came pouring in, but those who wanted to capitalize on Jones's appeal came face-to-face with Jones's integrity. The same man who could penalize himself one stroke in the U.S. Open refused hundreds of thousands of dollars worth of endorsements. There wasn't going to be any selling of Bobby Jones. The enterprises Jones selected reflected his good taste and his own enterprising spirit. Those ventures into which he entered, he would actively participate in.

He signed a contract with Warner Brothers to make a series of movie shorts. For the first series of twelve he was paid $120,000, plus a percent of the gross if the movies earned more than $360,000, which they did. For the second series of six he was paid $60,000. In all, Jones earned a quarter of a million dollars on these films; translated into today's buying power, that would be over $2 million.

The first series was entitled "How I Play Golf." Jones chose the title to avoid any notion that there was just one way to play or one formula to use. The series remains the finest species of its kind ever produced. For one thing, the films were directed by George Marshall, a very able craftsman who had directed Mack Sennett comedies and was himself a low handicap golfer. For another, no series of shorts ever had a greater cast. It included James Cagney, W. C. Fields, Edward G. Robinson, Loretta Young, Walter Huston, Joan Blondell, Frank Craven, Douglas Fairbanks, Jr., Richard Arlen, and Joe E. Brown, to name a few. The actors worked for nothing.

"We had a wonderful time," director Marshall said. "The

top actors and actress donated their time. All the stars were eager to take part. It was a privilege to have Jones work on their game."

Jones played himself. While not the easiest acting assignment, when compared to the strain of championship golf, it was relatively simple. He had a very pleasant natural voice and the stage presence of someone accustomed to being in the public eye. "Jones's voice records perfectly," reviewed *Film Daily*.

It was Jones's idea to start with the putter and work through the short irons to the long irons and then to the woods. "Jones didn't want a pretentious lecture on how golf should be played," remarked Marshall.

The dialogue was anything but, and Jones did enjoy himself. When asked if it had been fun, he said, "Hell, yes. I'll never forget it. There was a story line in each episode, but we didn't have a script—they made it up as we went along. The plots wound up at the end of each ten-minute short, and there was a lot of horseplay and comedy with the instructional business woven in."

Jones wrote all the instruction himself. O. B. Keeler did the narration of the shorts when necessary, and after each one he would say sententiously, "Watch for the next episode of Bobby Jones's 'How I Play Golf,' coming soon to your theater." In all, the shorts were shown in over 6,000 theaters and viewed by an estimated twenty-five million people.

Jones's next venture was to go on radio, at the same time his films were being released, for twenty-six weeks with O. B. Keeler—fifteen minutes every Wednesday evening sponsored by Listerine Shaving Cream. It was a re-creation of the high drama of Jones's career with some golf instruction thrown in. Listerine advertised their production in print: "Now your radio will help you battle par." It was carried nationally over NBC.

The other two projects Jones engaged in during 1931 proved memorable and durable; each carried the Jones signature as ingeniously as his brand of golf had.

For A. G. Spalding and Brothers, one of the top sporting goods firms in the United States, Jones helped design a new standard of golf club.

Up until that time, all the best irons had been made in Great Britain, with heads of hand-forged steel. Tom Stewart of St. Andrews, Scotland, was the supreme clubmaker, and it was from him that Jones accumulated over 200 clubs from which he tailored his own set of eighteen.

As yet, no American manufacturer had been able to duplicate the quality of the Scottish clubmaker. The irons produced in the United States were often much too long from heel to toe, and had a rather tinny feel when the golfer struck the ball, sending a mild shock up the hands and arms.

What Jones was after was the duplication of the sensation of his own irons, which gave a durable feeling, the sensation that one was actually squashing the ball. With the methodical J. Victor East of Spalding—who in the winter of 1930 reshafted Jones's driver, going through 5,000 pieces of first-grade hickory to get just the right one to give Jones the "feel" he wanted—and M. B. and W. F. Reach, Jones set out to duplicate his hickory-shafted clubs, but with steel shafts. The blade they came up with was more compact, with a thicker top line, and a flange sole was provided on the back of the head, bringing the center of gravity more nearly behind the direct center of the striking surface. Today the use of this flange is in some way present in all top-grade iron clubs.

The "Robert T. Jones, Jr." set of clubs came out in 1932.

Through the years Spalding sold over two million clubs in fifteen different models. They finally went off the market in 1973.

Of all the projects Jones engaged in during 1931, he brought the greatest fullness of his fertile mind and creative instincts to help found and codesign the course of the Augusta National Golf Club. While born out of Jones's desire to build his dream course, Augusta was also seeded by Jones's desire in 1930 to rediscover the joys of golf. In giving up championship golf, he wished to again experience the broader essence of the game—the fellowship that golf offers—under the more remote conditions of being just another member of a foursome, not a celebrity.

Impoverished nobility, a first-rate horticulturist, a New York City financier, the greatest golfer of his time, a great golf course architect—these together, a whole of glory turned and tooled, was what produced the Augusta National Golf Club.

In the fall of 1930, Clifford Roberts, a high-powered New York financier who had befriended Jones in the mid-1920s, and who tied himself as closely to Jones as he would to President Dwight Eisenhower in the 1950s, took Jones to the 365-acre tract of land in Augusta called Fruitlands. It had been a nursery owned since 1857 by the family of a Belgian baron, Louis Edouard Matheiu Berckmans. In the 1860s, the catalogue for Fruitlands listed as many as 1,300 varieties of pears and 900 types of apples.

It was the azalea bush, however, still seen in all its blazing glory each April at the Masters, that was the crowning work of the baron's son, Prosper, Fruitland's horticulturist. Prosper Berckmans realized the hardiness of the azalea and popularized it, thereby establishing what is probably Augusta's most important product.

When Roberts took Jones to the highest spot on the land overlooking two-thirds of the mildly rolling terrain, Jones realized he needn't look any further for where to build his "dream course." On this acreage he would help design for his beloved Southland a course to equal the best in the country.

The land had been put up for sale for the handsome price of $70,000 by the estate of Louis Berckmans's second wife. Roberts formed an underwriting group with the minimum commitment of $5,000 per person. The money was raised quickly. Despite this being the Depression, Jones's drawing power, the belief he elicited of limitless possibility, was as strong as ever.

Dr. Alister MacKenzie was hired as the architect; Jones was the codesigner. MacKenzie's theory on design was that a golf course should be as least artificial in appearance, and as much nature bound as possible. Such a course, he felt, would be more pleasurable to play and easier to maintain. To ensure this, Jones hit thousands of shots from every makeshift tee to every possible green. Such painstaking preparation also made sure the course would meet the high standards Jones had set for his own golf game.

As with so many great endeavors, the end product reflects the sum total of its creator's experience. Jones's signature is almost everywhere at Augusta National. The course shows so much of how Jones played golf, of his ingenious ability to know how to gauge a shot just so to get the ball close to the pin, along with his likes, his dislikes, and his fears.

Here are fairways so broad they seem almost impossible to miss, so few bunkers (only forty-four) they seem impossible to get into (not surprisingly, never have so few bunkers trapped so many balls), and greens so huge they seem impossible to miss. Where then are Jones's fears? Silly as it may seem, Jones

196

always harbored a terrible fear of looking foolish playing golf. He felt the average golfer, in some way, felt the same. Consequently, he and MacKenzie designed a course that would bring the most enjoyment for the greatest number of people. Of all the great golf courses in the United States, Augusta National is one of the fairest to the average golfer. And since Jones was a player who just couldn't forget a bad shot—he viewed a bad shot as its own penalty, thus is the conspicuous absence of so many hazards.

Because the strongest section of Jones's game always had been his fairway wood and his long and medium iron play, he designed a long course. And since he had a strong dislike for drive and pitch holes, from the championship tees Augusta National has only two par 4s under 400 yards.

"I have always said," Jones once remarked of the course, "that this can be a very easy course or a very tough one. There isn't a hole out there that can't be birdied if you just think. But there isn't one that can't be double-bogeyed if you stop thinking."

Here is Jones really commenting on his most prominent competitive golfing failing: his tendency to fall into mental complacency. The sheer largesse of Augusta National, with its some eighty acres of fairways and more than 101,000 square feet of greens (the average course has approximately thirty-five acres of fairways and 70,000 square feet of greens), is one of its *subtlest* features—a beguiling enticement to let the player's mind wander, to lose that vital concentration and hit a careless shot.

Few great players have given the carelessly hit shot more thought than Jones. He wrote of it: "One shot carelessly played can lead to a lot of grief. I think a careless shot invariably costs more than a bad shot painstakingly played, for it

197

leaves the morale in a state of disorder. It is easy to accept mistakes when we know that they could not be avoided. We realize that a good many shots must be less than perfect no matter how hard we try. But when we actually throw away strokes without rhyme or reason, it is pretty hard to accept the penalty philosophically and to attack the next shot in the proper frame of mind." All this Jones took into consideration when he helped design the course. Thus each hole must be played mentally from the green back to the tee. The drive must be judiciously played to accomplish the second objective: getting the ball close to the pin. Every approach shot demands the utmost in concentration and must be precisely struck, otherwise the ball will take an inconvenient bounce or two and roll unimpeded off the green or down one of the many humps in a green.

In 1932 the course was completed. It had met the fondest expectations of its designers. MacKenzie, who had seen it almost completed before he died in early 1932, called it "The World's Wonder Inland Course." Jones and Roberts believed it would be a great test for the best golfers in the country. Nonetheless, if it hadn't been for the reluctance of the USGA to offer the Open to Augusta, there might never have been the need to establish a championship known as the Masters, which has so wonderfully changed the face of championship golf in the world.

Jones and Roberts and other members of Augusta National conferred with the USGA in hopes of getting the U.S. Open, and that periodically the course would be a venue of the Open. Back and forth the topic went. Initially, for the USGA, it seemed ideal to hold the Open on a course codesigned by their favorite golfer, who had won more USGA championships than anyone else. And perhaps if there had been hardier strains of Bermuda grass or rye grass that wouldn't burn out in the summer heat, Augusta would have been awarded the Open. Unfortunately, not even Jones and Roberts could persuade the USGA to yield their position, that the Open continue to be played in June or July, rather than in the spring, when Augusta National literally was flowering in its best condition.

Roberts, who would rule and identify with Augusta National with the same arrogant pride with which Charles de Gaulle governed and identified with France, was undaunted, possessed as he was that his club have an annual tournament. His would differ from other tournaments in having Bobby Jones cast as its host and being built around Jones's only tournament appearance of the year.

The First Annual Invitation Tournament was held at Augusta National Golf Club, March 22 through 25, 1934. It had been Roberts's immediate idea to call the tournament the Masters, but Jones had vetoed this, feeling it would be presumptuous to call a tournament of their own creation the Masters. This was just one of many cases where Jones's modesty tempered Roberts's megalomania to give the tournament the quiet dignity and class it has.

Although the sportswriters themselves began calling the tournament the Masters, it wasn't until 1938 that this officially became its name. Even then, when asked about the name, Jones said, "I must admit it was born of a touch of immodesty."

Almost any time in March or April would have been appropriate for the tournament, with only a smattering of a winter golf tour still going on. The exact dates were chosen by Grantland Rice, a club member, who reasoned that in the last week in March the sportswriters would be drifting north after covering spring baseball training, and thus the press would be able to cover the tournament in full. Today the Masters is played the last four days of the first full week in April.

The first tournament offered a total prize of $5,000, with $1,500 going to the winner, or low professional. Second place was $800, and the remainder of the money was distributed over the next ten places. Jones wouldn't accept any money. "That is for the pros," he said. In all there were sixty-nine contestants, including ten amateurs.

For the first time in any important tournament, the prefix Mr. didn't precede an amateur's name, nor did it appear in front of Jones's name. No one objected. This was the first of so many firsts of tournament policies that were to be inaugurated at the Masters. Others to follow included the use of permanent towers for cameramen, the complete roping off of the fairways in the United States, now from tee all the way to the green, and the use of bleachers around certain greens other than the eighteenth. The Masters was also the first tournament to give the media its own first-rate working accommodations.

The 1934 Masters differed greatly from the Masters today. The qualification for being invited was less rigid. Invitations were sent to former U.S. Open or Amateur champions, British Open or Amateur champions, and members of the Walker or Ryder Cup teams. Some of those who were invited who were not nationally recognized players, but quite skillful, were just among Jones's very good friends.

The tournament was less ceremonial than it is now, with a sort of formal informality—something like an English lawn party where no one is introduced and no one cares. And gambling, though never sanctioned by Augusta National, was very

32. Literally as handsome as a movie star, Jones during his first stint in Hollywood.

33. On the set, Jones stars in the twelve-part movie series for Warner Brothers entitled "How I Play Golf." Seated is the director, George Marshall.

34. Jones with his family. Left to right: Bob Jones III, Clara, and Mary holding their youngest child, Mary Ellen.

35. Some of the Golden People of the Golden Age of Sport at the World's Champions Dinner sponsored by the Madison Square Garden Club. Top row, left to right: Babe Ruth, Gene Tunney, Johnny Weissmuller, and Bill Cook. Bottom row, left to right: Bill Tilden, Bobby Jones, Fred Spencer, and Charley Winters.

36. One of Jones's main enterprises after his retirement from competitive golf in 1930 was the founding and codesigning of the Augusta National Golf Club. Here he is seen hitting one of hundreds of drives to determine the exact location of the eighth tee.

37. Jones practices for the First Annual Invitation Tournament, as the original Masters was called in 1934.

38. "The Colonel," Jones's father, presents a
$1,500 check to Horton Smith, the winner of the
first Masters. Smith's winning score was 284.

39. Jones drives the first tee during the 1936 Masters as part of a notable foursome. Ready to play are
Gene Sarazen, Walter Hagen, and Tommy Armour. Between them, these four won thirty-two major
championships. Note Jones's huge thighs, the source of his power.

40. Jones with his good friend, and the most famous sportswriter of the time, Grantland Rice, returning from the 1936 Olympics.

41. A rare stop-action photograph of Jones at the moment of impact. Note how his head is behind the ball. The picture was taken for A. G. Spalding & Company, for whom Jones helped to design golf clubs, and for whom he later worked as a marketing executive.

42. Jones during World War II, a major in the U.S. Army Air Force.

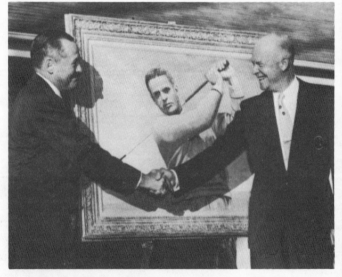

43. President Dwight Eisenhower presents Jones with a portrait he painted of him in 1953.

44. The only two American-born players to win four U.S. Opens: Jones and Ben Hogan, who won his fourth and final Open in 1953, the same year he captured the Masters and British Open.

45. Jones at age fifty-nine, permanently in a wheelchair and suffering from one of the rarest of neural diseases, syringomyelia. He fought it in vain and was slowly reduced to a helpless cripple.

much part of the scene. Before the tournament, at the Bon Air Vanderbilt, there were Calcutta pools, and for those who wanted more spirited betting there was Spec Reds, a gambling house, in the backwoods near the airport.

Jones was the main attraction of the first Masters. The odds were 6 to 1 he would win it. Although he neither confirmed nor denied that he was making a comeback, it was apparent to him after some dreadful putting the first two days that he no longer had the concentration or the will to undergo the punishment of championship golf. Henceforth, he made it clear that his role in the Masters would be as host, although he continued to play.

Horton Smith won the first tournament, ironically driving beautifully with none other than a Bobby Jones model driver from Spalding. Jones finished a dismal thirteenth, the highest he would ever finish in the Masters.

Next year, the nines were reversed. Jones felt that the present incoming nine holes with their perilous water hazards would provide more excitement as the final nine; they could torment a front-runner trying to protect his lead, and provide a player in the hunt with enough opportunities to gamble and make up ground.

Jones needed no more assurance that he was right than the 1935 Masters. Craig Wood sat in the clubhouse, the apparent winner with a score of six-under-par 282. Out on the par-5 fifteenth, with a pond fronting the green, Gene Sarazen stood on the fairway 220 yards away from the green needing three birdies to catch Wood. Feeling he had nothing to lose, Sarazen went for the green with his second shot, a 4-wood. He slashed into the ball and caught it flush. The ball cleared the pond, rolled onto the green, trickled slowly toward the pin, and dropped into the cup. A double eagle, one of the greatest shots ever hit in golf. In one hole Sarazen had caught Wood. He parred in and won the play-off.

Less than a dozen people witnessed the shot. Jones and Walter Hagen were two who did. Hagen was Sarazen's playing partner; Jones, as if directed by some magic instinct, had just wandered down to the fifteenth green.

The attendance at the Masters dropped terribly in its second year, to less than 10,000 spectators over four days. When the golfing population realized in 1934 that Jones wasn't going to reassert himself as "Emperor Jones," it just wasn't the same game of golf.

But if the Americans felt disillusioned about Jones, or at least had ceased to appreciate his beautiful swing for itself, the Scots hadn't.

In 1936 Bob and Mary Jones and Kit and Granny Rice went to Berlin to watch the Olympic games. On the way over they stopped in Scotland and stayed at the Gleneagles Hotel, not far from St. Andrews. On their last evening, Bob told Granny that he really couldn't bring himself so close to St. Andrews without playing the Old Course. Granny made arrangements the next day for a little informal luncheon in St. Andrews, then a casual round of golf for Bob with the pro, Willie Auchterlonie.

The luncheon went as expected, but not the golf. Word had gotten out that Jones was playing. When he arrived on the first tee, there were more than 5,000 people waiting, with 1,000 more still swarming onto the links. Shop owners closed their stores and posted signs reading "Our Bobby Is Back."

It was, for a while, time turned back. It could have been the 1927 British Open or the 1930 British Amateur, the way Jones played the front nine in just thirty-two shots, making four birdies. That he faltered on the back nine and finally scored a 71 didn't matter. It could have been an 80 or an 85. The important thing was "Our Bobby Is Back."

It was as if the citizens of St. Andrews had interpreted O. B. Keeler's final words on Jones's competitive career as a sort of litany.

Keeler earlier had written when Jones had retired: "And now it was goodbye to golf. And I could still say what I had said to people all over the world, that they could see for themselves if he was a golfer, but I could tell them that Bobby Jones was a much finer young man than he was a golfer. His great personality was paralleled only by his inimitable swing. Wholly lacking in affectation, modest to the degree of shyness, generous and thoughtful of his opponents, it is not likely that his equal will come again."

Jones would never play the Old Course again. Twenty-two years would pass before he revisited St. Andrews for one of the most stirring reunions in sport.

16

More often than not, when a sporting hero leaves the scene of his heroics, a new hero comes along. A beat isn't missed. It wasn't quite like that when Jones departed.

In 1931 Jones's wonderful friend, Francis Ouimet, won his second U.S. Amateur, seventeen years after he had captured his first one. He was thirty-eight at the time, and it was believed he didn't have the stamina for a week at match play.

The following year, Gene Sarazen captured the British Open and then, in the U.S. Open, played the last twenty-eight holes in 100 shots to win his second Open and become the first player since Jones to carry off the two national titles.

In 1934 and 1935, Lawson Little, a burly aggressive golfer, and one of the very best match players, pulled off a mini–Grand Slam by winning the U.S. and British Amateurs in two consecutive years for an incredible total of thirty-one consecutive matches.

All of these were great golfing heroes, but none had the hold on the golfing and non-golfing public that Jones had. Of course, it was their misfortune that their heroic feats took place during very hard times in America, as President Franklin Roosevelt held his hand over the heart of the Depression. Golf played among upper-class surroundings—clubhouses with indoor swimming pools, tennis courts, huge ballrooms, billiard rooms, bowling alleys; mammoth structures that appeared like unlaunched luxury liners—was very far from most people's minds. In these dark times even the name of Bobby Jones dimmed. For some he was viewed as a man from another era, as in fiction was Jay Gatsby.

For writers, however, the name Bobby Jones was still there with its usual diamond-hard brilliance. Without his ever being calculating, Jones's effect on the press was remarkable. In him they saw that the public and private man were much the same. He was as courteous off the course as he was on it. He had a wonderful warmth and spontaneity, plus that almost invaluable asset a public figure must have, an ability to remember people's names. He was intelligent but never pedantic. And within all this was wrapped a droll, self-deprecating sense of humor.

Jones smoked, sometimes to excess, drank, swore, and enjoyed telling a good dirty joke. He was almost totally lacking in pretension. "Pretension," Jones once exclaimed during the height of his golfing career, "what the hell is there to be pretentious about?"

In 1936, when Paul Gallico left the *Daily News* as its sports editor to write fiction, for which he is now most remembered, he wrote the classic sporting book, *Farewell to Sport*. His chapter on Jones was entitled "One Hero," and in it he wrote: "He was the only celebrity I ever knew who was prepared to accept as gracefully as possible every penalty there is to be paid for fame and publicity in the United States. . . . Well, what more can I say for my hero? He was a gentleman and there was laughter in his heart and on his lips, and he loved his friends."

To another writer, Bobby Jones epitomized the perfect American romantic individualist. The writer was F. Scott Fitzgerald.

During his final years working in Hollywood on movie scripts, and what would be his fine but unfinished novel about Hollywood, *The Last Tycoon,* Fitzgerald told his friends and his mistress, Sheilah Graham, that after his first novel, *This Side of Paradise,* was published, he had stolen his future wife, Zelda Sayre, away from the golfer, Bobby Jones.

When Andrew Turnbull was researching his excellent biography, *Scott Fitzgerald,* in the early 1960s, he wrote Jones to substantiate the point. Jones wrote back stating, yes, Zelda was in Atlanta for several years after World War I, and he had met her several times at parties. Again, Jones wished to avoid controversy. In truth, he was one of several young men in Atlanta at that time who were more than smitten over Zelda. And he was, as were the others, rejected for Scott.

Had Jones wanted, he could have kept his name sparkling in the public mind by giving exhibitions, but Jones wasn't the showman Hagen was. After he retired, Jones gave less than a dozen exhibitions, all for charitable causes. Jones could also have accepted hundreds of speaking engagements offered him. These he refused altogether. When he retired as a competitive golfer, he also retired as a public figure—which he had hated being—and concentrated on preserving his privacy.

In many ways, trying to keep up with the private Jones was almost as tough as battling him on the golf course. Although Jones hated pretension, he did enjoy living well; and by the late 1930s, he had become more than a moderately wealthy man. He had his large four-bedroom house on Tuxedo Road in Atlanta's northwest section, and a quaint summer home high up in the mountains in Highlands, North Carolina, a remote and enthrallingly beautiful area. Including part- and full-time help, he employed eight: a chauffeur, who sometimes served as a butler, a maid, a cook, a laundress, two nurses, a yardman, and a night watchman.

The watchman was hired in 1934 when fear gripped the Jones household. There had been a threat to kidnap Jones's son. The kidnapping of Charles Lindbergh's son in March 1932 was still fresh in people's minds as the long four-year trial continued. If not nationwide, at least still in the South, the name Bobby Jones was mentioned in the same breath as Robert E. Lee, Jefferson Davis, and Stonewall Jackson. Just how real the threat was remains obscure, but all protective caution was taken. The chauffeur, who drove the Jones children to Sacred Heart School, carried a gun, as did the watchman. The police knew the whereabouts of all the members of the Jones family at all times. The person who felt the worst about the whole matter was Jones's eldest daughter, Clara, whom Jones called "Sis." She felt humiliated that the kidnappers didn't want her.

While his concern for his children was genuine, Jones was a distant father. He had no great love for children, and his sense of paternal love only grew as his own children grew up. He had absolutely no tolerance for infant care. The man who could hold a putter so tenderly became seized with fright when holding a helpless infant.

Only when his children reached the age when they could intelligently converse did Jones become an active father, stern but immensely fair. When his children reached the age of eight and had acquired something close to civilized table manners, they were allowed to have dinner with their parents. Until they were almost teenagers, all the Jones children were raised by maids.

Mary was an aloof and strict mother, and her children were constantly subject to her quick and uncontrollable Irish temper. She was not above smacking her children into obedience. Thus, it was to their father rather than their mother that the Jones children went for solace and comfort. Under such circumstances, Jones was at his fatherly best. A man who never once laid a powerful hand on his children in anger, he spoke to them in his soft voice for as long as it took to make them see the reason why something should be done a particular way.

As his children grew older, Jones included them in many of his favorite activities, except golf. He took them to the opera and Georgia Tech football games, both of which Mary loathed.

Although none of his children inherited their father's love of opera, they did inherit, among other things, his penchant for swearing, which Jones mildly allowed. Fair being fair, he couldn't criticize his children for something he did. Once when his father visited the house on Tuxedo Road, he found Bob III playing on the front lawn and asked where his father was. "Oh," replied the four-year-old youngster, "Daddy is out back fixing the God damn lawn mower."

If Jones was short on infant and child care, he was long on reason and sense. The subject of golf was rarely discussed in the Jones household, and when his son announced that he wanted to learn golf, Jones had the great wisdom to try to discourage him, knowing that too much would be expected of him.

When Jones's attempts at dissuasion failed, he took a new

approach. He notified his own teacher, Stewart Maiden, and asked him to give Bob III a lesson—one that would discourage him from taking up the game. Jones believed it would be a simple task for the canny Scot. Maiden requested that Bob III be on the practice tee at East Lake at 8:30 A.M. The youngster arrived promptly. He was still taking his lesson and hitting hundreds of practice shots by noon, at which time he put down his 5-iron, and began walking toward the clubhouse.

"Laddie, where do you think you're going?" asked Maiden.

"To have lunch," replied the boy.

"Come back here," demanded Maiden. "I don't have lunch."

So with his hands blistered and bloody, the youngster was finally excused from the practice at 4:30 P.M.

Even so, Bob III persisted. Frustration followed frustration. He did win the Atlanta City Junior Championship in 1941, and several club championships, but that was it. He qualified for three U.S. Amateurs, but never made it past the first round. He played in his last U.S. Amateur in 1959 when, in the first round, in a stroke of prophetic irony, he lost 7 and 6 to an eighteen-year-old named Jack Nicklaus.

The downfall of young Bob's game was what had almost been the downfall of his father's game—the inability to control a horrible temper. He was forever goddamning every missed shot.

He was to remain all his life a most dissatisfied golfer. Although he realized he did not have his father's genius for the game, he felt nevertheless that being the son of Bobby Jones he should play better than he did. In this way, he was a bit like his grandfather, The Colonel, who always felt he should have been better than an eighty-shooter. Big Bob never could comprehend it—after all, hadn't he helped produce one of the greatest of golfers. It was never his fault when he shot a bad round; it was his clubs, the weather, or the condition of the course. He was forever hunting for some magic secret, even into his fifties. During the golf season in the late 1930s, there was hardly a Monday morning when he didn't come into his son's office at the law firm of Jones, Powers and Williams at the Citizens Southern Bank, and espouse a new theory on the golf swing.

At the time, Bob was only a nominal partner in the firm; he no longer was practicing the nitty-gritty of corporate law and, although he could have, he declined to draw a salary.

Jones's business interests were diverse and profitable. He was now a vice president for A. G. Spalding. In early 1939, he purchased from the Coca-Cola Company a franchise to bottle and distribute Coca-Cola in New England. It was one of the very first plants in the area going north from Pittsfield, Massachusetts, to Brandon, Vermont, and it was the first of Jones's many interests as a Coca-Cola bottler.

It was no mere coincidence that Jones's first involvement as a Coca-Cola bottler occurred around the time one of his regular Sunday morning golfing companions, Robert W. Woodruff, became the board chairman and executive committee chairman of the Coca-Cola Company. Woodruff was a man who never went beyond high school and became one of the greatest business tycoons in America. Such has been his financial and personal influence in Atlanta that he has often been referred to as "a quorum of one."

With the advent of World War II, Woodruff seized the opportunity to further expand the international division of Coca-Cola. He issued a directive to the War Department: "We will see that every man in uniform gets a bottle of Coca-Cola for five cents where he is and whatever it costs."

A total of sixty-four bottling plants was shipped around the world.

Bobby Jones didn't have to go to war. In 1941 when the United States declared war on Japan and the European Axis, he was thirty-nine years old with a medical disability. Because of a serious varicose vein condition (he had undergone a second operation in 1934 during which several veins in his legs had been tied off), he actually qualified as 4-F. He was also married and the father of three children.

Regardless of his status, there was never a question in Jones's mind as to whether he should be directly, militarily involved in the war effort. For someone who had to accept so many responsibilities, it was just one more consistent step. And war did appeal to his competitive instincts, far more than the probable prospects of being an entertainer giving golfing exhibitions to sell war bonds, as Bob Hope and Bing Crosby did so successfully. After receiving a waiver for medical reasons, Jones volunteered for the United States Air Force. In early 1942, he was inducted as a captain.

Jones was put into the U.S. Army Air Force's intelligence corps and sent to Harrisburg, Pennsylvania, for ten weeks of intensified training. He learned aerial photographic interpretation, navigation, and the tactics and techniques of scattered and saturated bombings. More specifically, Jones, the man who as a competitive golfer could look an opponent in the eye on the first tee and size him up, was trained as a prisoner interrogator.

Jones was assigned to the Ninth Air Force, some units of which, by 1943, were flying daring daytime bombing raids over Germany. After badgering several commanding officers, most of whom wanted him in the States, Jones got his wish and was sent overseas to be stationed at an air force base on the north-western coast of England. He now had been promoted to Major. By early spring 1944, the Ninth Air Force had reduced most of its air strikes, and the unit was put directly under the command of General Dwight Eisenhower. The preparation of D-Day was almost complete.

On April 8, 1944, Jones wrote his eldest daughter, Clara. He couldn't write about the war; in fact, the tone of the letter was as if he was safely back at his desk in an office in the Pentagon.

My dearest girl,

Ten days from now will be your nineteenth birthday! My, it's hard to believe, mainly because I don't feel that old. Yet I'm glad to see you growing up. You have meant so much more to me as a young lady than you did as a child. One of the things I want to do most now is to get back so I can enjoy being with you some more.

I do hope you have a happy birthday, darling, not because one happy day means so very much, but because if you're happy one day you're likely to be happy most of the time before and after.

I wish I could send you a nice present, but I'm afraid I'll have to leave it to Mom to count me in on hers. There just isn't anything to buy here, and if there were, I doubt if I could find time to look for it.

Sweet, I hope this reaches you before your birthday, but if it should not, remember I was thinking of you then and lots of other times.

> Worlds of love and congratulations,
> Devotedly,
>
> Dad

Two months later, on June 7, D-Day plus one, Jones and his unit were burrowed deep in foxholes on a beach in Normandy, where they spent two days and nights under sporadic enemy artillery fire. Jones would spend only a few months near the front lines, for in the late fall of 1944, he was mustered out of the Army Air Force with the rank of Lieutenant Colonel.

While he had been away, his mother, whom his children called "Granny," and The Colonel had moved temporarily into Jones's house to help Mary take care of the children. Clara and her husband had long since stopped sharing the same bedroom, and she pretty much ran her daughter-in-law's house as she did her own, from her bedroom. She was suffering, as she had been for the last ten years, from pernicious anemia. She had become a woman who enjoyed poor health.

By contrast, her son—except for the loss of twenty pounds— was the picture of perfect health. At forty-three, as in his youth, there was a restrained aura of vitality and power about him. His hair had darkened and begun to recede, but his pale blue-gray eyes still had a mysterious quality to them. A small network of crow's-feet marched toward his temple, where there was just a smattering of gray hairs. His face was fuller, but there was no softness to it. If anything, he looked even more square-jawed. He was aging well, and looking very much like the wise, mature statesman. In the next decade he would age twenty years.

Jones resumed his business as vice president for A. G. Spalding Company and made plans to expand his Coca-Cola bottling operations. With his good friend, Dick Carlington, Jones founded Peachtree Golf Club in Atlanta. He hired another Jones—Robert Trent Jones—to design the course.

Jones had also returned as president of Augusta National Golf Club, which meant that it was his and Cliff Roberts's responsibility to get the course back into shape.

The last prewar Masters had been played in April 1942. It had been the best championship to date. At the halfway mark, Ben Hogan was eight shots behind his rival from Fort Worth,

Texas, Byron Nelson. Nelson had already won a U.S. Open, a PGA Championship, and the 1937 Masters. Hogan caught Nelson and, in the play-off, after five holes, had a three-shot lead. Then Nelson's iron game—he was one of the best iron players the game has known—got hot. Over a stretch of eleven holes, most of it over the perilous back nine, Nelson picked up five shots on Hogan, who played the same stretch of holes in one under, to win by one shot.

The course and club were closed down shortly after the tournament, until early 1945. Hoping to save money, the members of the club bought a herd of Herefords, which grazed over the once lush fairways. When a photo of the herd appeared in *Time* magazine, the caption read, "End of a Golfer's Dream."

It almost was. Besides the fairways, the Herefords also grazed on the azaleas and other flora. It took six months and forty-two German prisoners of war, hired by the club from nearby Camp Gordon, to get the course back in shape. The first postwar Masters was played in April 1946, and again Hogan was very much in the fight. He came to the final hole needing a birdie to win, a par to tie. He struck a 5-iron shot, and the ball stopped twenty feet above the pin. Boldly, Hogan went for his birdie, and the ball slipped three feet past. He missed it coming back. Herman Keiser won and picked up first-prize money, upped from $5,000 to $10,000.

After two rounds of the 1947 Masters, Bobby Jones withdrew. The soreness in his neck and shoulders had become too painful for him to swing. He was sure it was nothing too serious, just a flaring up of bursitis. He had experienced "cricks" in his neck on and off since 1926. "Boys," he told his golfing friends, "I'll join you on the first tee next year."

17

Bobby Jones would die by inches and suffer by yards.

On July 9, 1956, Jones flew into New York City's Idlewild Airport. It was a hot and muggy day, not unlike the day almost exactly twenty-six years before when, as the conqueror of the British Amateur and Open, he had been driven up lower Broadway among a swirling of ticker tape. Then a vigorous young man, he held the promise of limitless possibility.

Now he was alone, going through the old Idlewild Airport. There were no autograph seekers, not one photographer or reporter. Jones looked like any other busy businessman, dressed in a light gray suit, a blue shirt, and a striped tie. He would have gone completely unnoticed except for the fact that he wore a brace on his right leg and walked with a slow shuffling motion with two canes. His face had taken on a rather heavy jowly appearance from the cortisone he was taking. Still, he looked very distinguished when sitting and smoking his cigarettes from a black ivory cigarette holder, a protection rather than an affectation. Since 1953, Jones had repeatedly burned his fingers, feeling little of the skin-searing heat from his cigarette.

Medically, New York City was Jones's last stop. For the next five days, he would be thoroughly examined by Dr. H. Houston Merritt, chairman of the Department of Neurology, dean of the College of Physicians and Surgeons at the Columbia-Presbyterian Medical Center, the man who first used Dilantin to treat epilepsy.

Jones had been unable to keep his promise at the end of the 1947 Masters. Since then he had come under the surgeon's knife twice. The back of his neck was a network of ugly scar tissue. The operations, each of which Jones considered a panacea to a weakening in his legs and a slight atrophying condition in his right arm, had been in vain.

In November 1948, at Emory University Hospital in Atlanta, Jones had undergone a delicate operation for an abnormal bone growth on the fourth, fifth, and sixth cervical vertebrae, a growth that was believed to be pressing on a nerve and causing his condition. So dangerous is the operation that one wrong cut by the surgeon's knife can paralyze a patient from the neck down.

The bone growth was successfully removed; yet Jones continued to have a certain spasticity and numbness in his right leg and difficulty using his right arm. Over the next two years, Jones experienced the same sensations on his left side. In May 1950, he went to the Lahey Clinic in Boston for another operation to relieve what was considered a damaged disc, believed to be pressing on a nerve. As with the first operation, it was futile. Up until that time, no one had considered Jones's problem to be one that could not be cured surgically.

In 1956 Jones's physician, Dr. Frank M. Atkins, recommended that he see Dr. H. Houston Merritt. Jones, the man who considered the preparation of a golf shot as important as the shot itself, prepared for the examination in the same way, leaving nothing to chance. He had all his medical records sent to Dr. Merritt, then wrote him on June 25, 1956:

"You said on the phone that you 'have a bed for me.' I hope you will be able to get a private room with a bath and telephone. I am grateful for the opportunity of talking to you this morning and am very eager to have you look me over. I have a feeling that I am going downhill, and will be pleased if this reverse progress can only be arrested . . ."

On July 3, Jones again wrote Dr. Merritt:

"For the record, I might add two notes which may or may not be of importance. I experienced a moderate coronary thrombosis in the fall of 1952, and was under the care of Dr. Bruce Logue. Dr. Atkins tells me that Dr. Logue has said there are no contraindications with respect to an anesthetic, in the event you should care to do a spinal puncture.

"On two occasions, I have had quite unpleasant reactions from penicillin . . ."

On July 13, 1956, Jones was discharged from the Neurological Institute of the Columbia-Presbyterian Medical Center. Dr. Merritt filed a two-and-a-half-page medical report, parts of which are summarized as follows:

Chief Complaint: Difficulty in using both hands and legs, progressively over an 8-year period.

Present Illness: This is the first Neurological Institute of New York admission of a 54-year-old right-handed lawyer, formerly a golf amateur. The patient had been in excellent health

until 1948 when he developed double vision for distant objects. For example, a
distant green would appear double, but a
golf ball directly in front of him would
not. This episode lasted 6 weeks.

In May 1948, the patient noticed difficulty in the use of his right hand and began stubbing his right foot. When he
would swing a golf club, he would experience a burning feeling down the left side
of his body. The difficulty in using the
right arm and leg progressed so that by
July 1948 the patient was unable to play
golf. . . .

Since 1950 there has been slow progres-
sion so that the patient has had to use leg
braces and canes walking. Wasting of the
intrinsic muscles of both hands, but especially the right, has been noted by the patient. Recently the patient has found it
difficult to perceive hot and cold with his
hands. . . .

Neurological   The gait is spastic with greater stiffness of
Examination: the right leg. There is moderately severe
atrophy of the interossei of both hands
especially on the right. The right mid-
thigh is 3 cm. smaller than the left. There
is definite weakness of the triceps, the
forearm and hand muscles bilaterally.
Weakness of the muscles of the trunk and
of both lower extremities right more than
left is present. The patient is unable to
dorsiflex his right foot.

225

Sensory Examination: Pain and temperature are impaired bilaterally over the dermatomes . . . Light
touch is mildly impaired in both hands.
Position sense is normal. There is slight
decrease in vibratory sense in the lower
extremities. Cranial nerve examinations
within normal limits.

Course in Hospital: The history and finding were felt to be
consistent with the diagnosis of syringo-
myelia.

Bobby Jones would call the disease hell.

Technically, syringomyelia is a disease of the spinal cord in
which a cavitation develops, usually in the cervical area. Although it can rarely be arrested, it is almost always progressive.
As the cavitation enlarges, there is severe damage to the sensory and motor nerves. Eventually, the victim loses all feeling
of pain and temperature in the extremities. As the motor
nerves are damaged, atrophy occurs and the muscles waste
away. There is severe loss of coordination. Paradoxically, while
the disease destroys sensory feeling, it produces a constant
deep aching pain, usually in the neck or upper arms.

The origin of syringomyelia is believed to be congenital,
although not hereditary. There is no universal cure or treat-
ment of it. The disease doesn't affect a victim's intellect, hear-
ing or vision, and in itself isn't terminal. Indirectly, however, it
kills most middle-age victims in twelve to fifteen years. It took
twenty-three years to kill Bobby Jones.

Whenever Jones was questioned by the general press about
his condition, he presented a rather reconciled manner. "Re-

member," he would say, "we play the ball as it lies." Just the opposite was the truth.

Early one morning he woke up without remembering he could hardly walk, stepped out of bed to go to the bathroom, and fell flat on his face. There he lay for ten minutes, cursing madly and beating the floor with his fists.

In 1951 he told the story to his old and dear childhood friend, Alexa Stirling, who in the early 1920s had gotten married and moved to Ottawa, Canada. She had come to visit for the fiftieth anniversary of the Atlanta Athletic Club. Jones finished relating the story with his wry sense of humor, then added, "For ten minutes nobody dared come near me. I would have bitten them."

Alexa listened compassionately and then said, "Bob, if you can laugh at yourself, it certainly shows you've made an adjustment to this condition."

"Adjustment?" Jones said angrily. "If adjustment means acceptance, I'd say no. I still can't accept this thing; I fight it every day. When it first happened to me I was pretty bitter, and there were times when I didn't want to go on living. But I did go on living, so I had to face the problem of how I was going to live. I decided I'd just do the very best I could."

When Jones was winning national championships, he sincerely told the press that he didn't think he was a better player than some of the others: he simply tried harder. Years hadn't dulled his competitive edge, and he'd be damned if he would accept any soupy sympathy, or be treated as a cripple.

In 1952 Jones, up until then a registered Democrat, switched parties and served as chairman of the Georgia committee to elect Dwight Eisenhower President. For the first time since the Civil War, Georgia went Republican. Jones also took up bridge, taking more lessons at the game than he ever did at golf. Some were from the master himself, Charles Goren. Even with a brace on his leg, Jones still attempted to play golf, although he couldn't pivot and had to keep most of his weight on his left leg. One day at Augusta National, he parred the eighteenth hole, using a driver off the tee, two 3-wood shots, and finally chipping for his four. When healthy he had usually played the hole with a driver and 7-iron.

Jones continued as host of the Masters and, as the club's president, always presided over the presentation ceremonies. More and more he began to be looked upon as the senior statesman of golf. As each April came, when Jones made his appearance at the Masters, often holding court in his cottage east of the tenth green, the tournament began to take on a sort of intensified gathering of the clan, something of an unofficial signal that the golf season had arrived, along with the renewal of hope that accompanies spring.

The Masters was still considered a magnificently run invitational tournament. As yet, it didn't have the status of a major championship.

Historically, 1954 remains the year when the Masters took on a truer meaning and became the sixth major golf championship along with the U.S. Open and Amateur, the British Open and Amateur, and the PGA Championship. The time was right. The circumstances were ideal. President Dwight Eisenhower, himself a regular member of Augusta National since 1948, made no secret of his love of golf and his great respect and affection for Bobby Jones. A whole nation had become aware of what Ike shot, or what he liked to tell the press: "Don't ask what I shot."

One of Ike's financial advisors was Clifford Roberts. There

228

was even a special cabin, now known as "Mamie's Cabin," built at Augusta National for the President's frequent visits.

Then there was the 1954 Masters, truly the most memorable to date. An amateur, Billy Joe Patton, came within one stroke of tying the two best players in the world. At the end of regulation play, Sam Snead, the man who swings the golf club as it ought to be swung, and Ben Hogan, the finest striker of the ball in golf, who the previous year had won the Masters, and the U.S. and British Open, were tied. Snead beat Hogan by a single shot in the play-off.

That fall, a young man who kept hitching up his trousers and who couldn't keep his shirttail in won the U.S. Amateur. He was Arnold Daniel Palmer. A golf boom was on.

In 1956 the Masters was first televised over CBS, as it has continued to be. Roberts wanted only the most prestigious firms to advertise. Cadillac Motors was one. With his tremendous financial influence, Roberts simply called up Don E. Ahrens, president of Cadillac, and told him they were going to be one of the television advertisers. That was that.

The Masters has been called many wonderful things. The most flowery compliment it has received was written by Bill Sixty in the *Milwaukee Journal*: "The Masters is the aristocrat of golf—the acme of color, refinement and fan appeal. It rises aloof and alone above the rest."

Time and again, the Masters' gallery is considered the best-behaved in the world. This didn't just happen.

Although by 1967 Jones was too sick even to go out on the course in a golf car, he could watch some of the play from his cabin off the tenth tee. During the second round, Jack Nicklaus, still being called "Fat Jack," and playing under the shadow of a gallery-worshiped Arnold Palmer, was cheered when he missed a putt. When Jones heard of the incident, he was furious. He immediately wrote a message that still appears on every admission ticket:

In golf, customs of etiquette and decorum are just as important as rules governing play. It is appropriate for spectators to applaud successful strokes in proportion to difficulty, but excess demonstrations by a player or partisans are not proper because of the possible effect upon other competitors.

Most distressing to those who love the game of golf is the applauding or cheering of misplays or misfortunes of a player. Such occurrences have been rare at the Masters, but we must eliminate them entirely if our patrons are to continue to merit their reputation as the most knowledgeable and considerate in the world.

SUGGESTIONS

No matter how well you may know a player, do not accost him on the golf course. Give him a chance to concentrate on his game.

Walk—never run. Be silent and motionless when a contestant prepares to execute a stroke. Be considerate of other spectators. Golf is a gentleman's game.

Only a championship golfer could have written such an effective note. One had to know the unexplainable ebb and flow of a player's confidence, how a sharp movement in the gallery can distract a player, and how some untimely noise can break a player's concentration. Also, the brevity of the note, the lack of even one needless word, its perfect structure, are all indicative of an author with an excellent command of the English language.

Although Jones had given up his column on golf in 1935, he was under contract in 1957 with Doubleday and Company to write a second autobiography, his account of his golfing life, the Grand Slam, and the story of Augusta National Golf Club and the Masters.

Painstakingly, he began writing on a long legal yellow pad, but because the muscles of his hand contracted so much, he finally resorted to a dictating machine. After each chapter was typed, he went over it word for word. He finished the 70,000-word manuscript in the late spring of 1959. In March 1960, *Golf Is My Game* by Robert Tyre (Bobby) Jones was published. It received very favorable reviews on its style and content, sold over 35,000 copies, and went into two printings.

That fall, *Sports Illustrated* wanted to publish two chapters from *Golf Is My Game*. They agreed to pay $5,000 for second North American serial rights. When Jones's editor at Doubleday, Ferris Mack, was informed of the option, he called to discuss the matter with Jones. Upon hearing the fee, Jones said, "I wouldn't walk across the God damn street for five thousand dollars. Make it ten thousand . . ." *Sports Illustrated* agreed and ran the two chapters in their November 7 and 14 issues.

In the book, Jones imparted more of his golfing wisdom, answering that often murky question, why golf, of so many games, attracts so many people whose careers are constantly filled with important decision making.

"Golf," wrote Jones, "has a very great and sometimes mystifying appeal to busy men. Some of its most ardent devotees are men of affairs whose lives are filled with responsibilities for making important decisions. To those who know little of golf, it is difficult to explain how a game so apparently frivolous could interest men such as these.

"To those who know something of the game, there is no mystery at all. Golfers know, and have known for a long time, that when playing golf, it is almost impossible to think of anything else. The most complete rest of the mind, the most effective renewal of mental keenness and vigor, come not from thinking of nothing, but from putting one's mind completely upon fresh and stimulating activities. It is, therefore, the all-absorbing challenge of golf which makes it such an effective agent of mental therapy."

Although Jones no longer could even grip a golf club, he still held a deep and passionate love for the game. He continued, as he had since 1937, to be committeeman on the United States Golf Association's museum committee. In 1958 he served as nonplaying captain for the U.S. team in the inaugural World Cup matches. From time to time he would, without the slightest fanfare, show up at national championships and watch play from a golf car.

Jack Nicklaus, whose idol has always been Bobby Jones, still recalls the minor fear he felt when playing in his first U.S. Amateur in 1955 at The Country Club of Virginia. For several holes, there was Jones in a golf car, watching the fifteen-year-old. Nicklaus became so nervous playing in the presence of Jones, he mis-hit every shot. He was defeated 1 up in the first round.

In all, Jones wore the crown of the senior statesman in golf with all the modesty, dignity, and humor with which he had worn the crown of best golfer in the world in the 1920s. Never once did he show any measure of jealousy or put down the deeds of the newer breed of players. In 1953, after Hogan had captured the British Open to add to the fourth U.S. Open he had won that year and his second Masters title, Jones happened to be in New York City on business and was invited to sit on the dais for a luncheon at the Waldorf-Astoria honoring

Hogan. There was a swirling of controversy among the sportswriters as to who was the better golfer, Jones or Hogan. Jones
realized the importance of the situation and spoke privately to
Hogan. "Ben," he said, "I want you to understand very clearly
that I had nothing to do with the controversial stories about
you and me, and I certainly didn't project myself in the picture with any idea of detracting from your enjoyment of the
glory which you've earned."

Unlike Tilden, who always was at war with the governing
body of his sport, the United States Lawn Tennis Association,
particularly over his amateur status, Jones carried on an almost
perfect marriage with the USGA. He was an executive committeeman in 1928, 1929, and 1930. In 1948 he was honorary
chairman of the USGA Public Links championship. In 1955
the USGA set up the Bob Jones Award for distinguished
sportsmanship in golf. Significantly, its first recipient was
Jones's wonderful friend, Francis Ouimet. Eventually, Jones
donated all his medals and trophies, and his beloved putter,
Calamity Jane, to the USGA.

In 1962, Joseph C. Dey, then executive director of the
USGA, made Jones the friendly gesture of sending him an
application for reinstatement of his full amateur status. Since
1930 Jones had been classified as an ex-amateur, or as the
USGA called it, nonamateur. Dey sent the standard USGA
printed form, and Jones responded with good humor.

To the question, Present occupation? Jones wrote, "Assistant."

Employer? Jones answered, "Clifford Roberts."

To the question, Do you understand the Rules of Amateur
Status? Jones wrote, "No."

To the following question: Without any mental reservations, have you decided permanently to abandon all activities contrary to those rules? Jones answered, "I have no mental reservations about anything."

It was a wonder that Jones could still see the light side of life, for in his own life the center wasn't holding. Besides his own horrible deteriorating condition, Jones's dedicated physician, Dr. Ralph Murphy, discovered in 1961 that Mary Jones had cancer of the larynx. Fortunately, it was discovered soon enough and, after a half-year of radiotherapy treatments, the condition was arrested.

Now Jones was relying more and more on a wheelchair. Although he still could walk with his two canes and leg braces, it would take him almost ten minutes to go fifty yards. The muscles in his hands had wasted away and contracted so that his hands were now distorted into an almost petrified clawlike position, and he no longer could feel any temperature in them.

He knew his condition could only get worse. But not quite yet was Jones going to let the disease get the better of him. He still had that indomitable will to live, and to live in dignity.

He still went to work every day. He had by now hired a large and kind black man named George Hoyt to tend to his needs. Every morning Hoyt shaved and dressed Jones, and then drove him to his office at the law firm of Jones, Bird and Howell, in the Haas Howell Building on Poplar Street, so centrally located in Atlanta it surely was one of the original wagon tracks when the city was known as Terminus.

Jones now labored in what one of his law partners called "the vineyards of the law." After Jones's father, "Colonel Bob," died in 1956, the law firm of Jones, Williams, Dorsey was incorporated into the Bird and Howell law firm. Jones took over his father's former duties of handling the legal work for the Jones Mercantile Company and the Canton Textile Mills; he was on the board of directors of both companies and had large financial holdings.

But it was Jones's interest as a bottler and distributor of Coca-Cola that led many of his admirers to believe he was a millionaire many, many times over. He was not.

Altogether his net worth was over $2 million. He carried a half-million-dollar life insurance policy and lived in an expensive Venetian-style house called "Whitehall" on Tuxedo Road, a house filled with a valuable collection of English and American antiques and a very valuable porcelain collection which he and Mary had added to over the years. Each had a Fleetwood Cadillac, and they still had three in help. From 1956 until his death, Jones's yearly income—partly from his Coca-Cola interest, his royalties and stock from A. G. Spalding, and his earnings from the law firm, and mainly from his interest from the Canton Textile Mills—ranged from $75,000 to slightly over $100,000.

It should have been much more. As a businessman, Jones was as straight as an arrow, with a strong sense of fair play. He expected the same from other people, never acknowledging there was any other way of doing business.

Being the major stockholder of a Coca-Cola bottling and distributing plant in Eau Claire, Wisconsin, Jones installed his brother-in-law as manager; in the late 1950s he had to sell out for less than $25,000, an amount he considered sinful. For his plant in Pittsfield, Massachusetts, Jones installed his son as manager. The plant never yielded more than a $100,000 annual profit, most of which was reinvested into the business.

Still, Jones believed in Coca-Cola as Texans believe in oil.

In the mid-1950s, Jones sold out his interest in a syndicate that he and seven other men had formed to purchase 25 percent of a bottling plant in Glasgow, Scotland. Jones got no more than his original investment back.

In South America it was different. In 1945 Jones had invested $7,000, along with thirty other men—including Clifford Roberts—to form a syndicate that bought 40 percent of three Latin American bottling plants in Uruguay, Argentina, and Chile. Business boomed, but never was a dividend paid. All profits were reinvested to expand the plants. In the late 1950s, Uruguay's plant ranked twelfth among all of Coca-Cola's export operations. In 1962 Jones sold his interest for over $100,000.

In 1970 he sold his plant in Pittsfield—land, equipment, and all—for $1.25 million. Most of the money went to Mary and the children, for each of whom Jones had set up trust funds. The rest went for medical expenses, which continued to soar at an astronomical rate. Since 1964, Jones had been practically a paraplegic, permanently implanted in a wheelchair. Besides George Hoyt, he employed an evening nurse. He was sixty-two, but looked at least seventy-two. There was a constant puffiness beneath his eyes from the hours of sleepless nights; his once perpetually bronze face now had a rather gray color to it. The years of medication had dissipated his once handsome looks.

Year after year, as Jones continued to go to the Masters and preside at the presentation ceremonies on television, a nation of golfers, many of whom had never seen Jones in his prime, couldn't quite comprehend that this man had once conquered all the worlds there were to conquer in golf. Or perhaps it was just the narrow mentality of a jaded sporting world, a condescending notion that the Golden People of the Golden Age of Sport, like chimney sweeps, turn to dust.

Ferris Mack, a senior editor at Doubleday and Company,

didn't see it that way. In 1964 he signed Jones to another book contract. This time it was to be a collection of instructional pieces Jones had written between 1927 and 1935. The book would take on the title of his columns, *Bobby Jones on Golf.* Jones hired one of his good friends, an excellent writer and keen golfing historian named Charlie Price, to edit the pieces. Price had been the first editor of *Golf World* and *Golf Magazine,* and his first-rate book, *The World of Golf,* which Jones foreworded, remains a classic on the history of the game.

It was Price's job to go through the nearly 300,000 words Jones had written and reduce them to 80,000. As Price wrote in his foreword, "Almost any eighty thousand words would have made a better book on golf than I have ever read before. Since all of these columns were unfailingly articulate, what I tried to save from each was the timeless . . .

"When I was through with what I thought was a masterpiece, Jones then took the manuscript and, over a period of months, picked apart every chapter, every paragraph and every sentence, every phrase of his own writing until he was sure that thirty years had not dimmed what he had truly meant to say. . . ." The book, published in 1966, sold more than 25,000 copies and, as with *Golf Is My Game,* was highly praised.

In 1968 Bobby Jones made his last appearance at the Masters. Even though he was almost a quadriplegic by now, he continued to hold court in his cottage by the tenth tee. As usual, he refused to talk about his illness. Indeed, only a very few people really knew just how sick he was, how much suffering he had endured, and how in twenty years syringomyelia had not only left him a helpless cripple, but now was breaking down that seemingly indomitable will to live.

On September 10, 1968, Jones wrote Dr. H. Houston Merritt at Columbia-Presbyterian Medical Center.

Dear Dr. Merritt:

You may recall that in 1956 you diagnosed me as a likely victim of Syringomyelia. On July 17th, 1956, you wrote my doctor, Dr. F. M. Atkins, saying that this is a "slowly progressive disease with a relatively good prognosis as far as length of life is concerned."

I hope you will appreciate that I am saying this with all the good humor of which I am capable, but I am getting pretty fed up with this "relatively good prognosis." My life day and night is about as nearly miserable as one could imagine. I am not in any great pain, but experience constant discomfort in all members in all postures.

Naturally, the first thing I am interested in is a way to become more comfortable. My mobility is already practically nil, since I am confined to a wheelchair and have no useful function in my left arm. . . .

I am sixty-six years old. I have wasted away to a bare skeleton and keep going only with the aid of three or four devoted people. I have chronic asthmatic bronchitis, a low blood pressure, and for several years have been wearing a permanent catheter because of a slight prostate enlargement. . . .

Two days later Jones wrote his own physician, Dr. Ralph Murphy.

Dear Ralph:

. . . This letter will indicate to you what is on my mind and what I want to discuss seriously with you. I have a very real horror of spending my final years lying paralyzed or in twisted agony. Any other way out, no matter how quickly it comes, would be better. I am sure you will agree.

Of how Jones got through his last three and a half years his physician would simply write, "I suppose it was a tribute to his inner competitive spirit."

Jones was to realize his worst horror. From April to December 1971, he was confined to his bed, able to get up only a few hours each day. On December 4, 1971, the aneurysm of the abdominal aorta (found three years earlier) ruptured. It probably would have killed most people in Jones's condition in less than a week; it took two and a half weeks to kill Jones. On December 10, mostly in a gesture to please Mary, Jones took the vows converting to Catholicism, with Monsignor McDonaugh of Atlanta's Christ the King Cathedral performing the service. Afterward, Jones asked the Monsignor to stay for a drink. Sipping his Scotch and water from a straw, Jones said to the Monsignor, "You know, if I'd known how happy this has made Mary, I would have done it years ago."

At 6:33 P.M. on December 18, Bobby Jones died peacefully in his sleep at home. At his bedside were his wife and children.

His grave at the Oakland Cemetery is near an old brick wall, partially shaded by a huge ancient oak tree. His tombstone of white Georgian marble simply reads: ROBERT TYRE JONES, JR. BORN 1902, DIED 1971.

On Thursday, May 4, 1972, at noon, there was "A Service of Thanksgiving and Commemoration for Robert Tyre Jones," at the Parish Church of the Holy Trinity in St. Andrews, Scotland. The address was given by Roger Wethered, Esq., whom Jones had beaten in the finals of the 1930 British Amateur.

Wethered concluded his address saying, "To have won through at golf after those years when nothing would quite come right was an epic victory in itself, but the second victory—the one in which he was reduced to walking with difficulty with a cane and finally to a wheelchair—was a victory of the spirit that will also live as long as his name is remembered."

Jones was almost as powerful in death as in life. To his family he was. They believed in the literal interpretation of the Book of St. John in the New Testament, "In my Father's house are many mansions . . ." The house was gone.

After he died, Mary Jones became more and more despondent and fell into occasional spells of heavy drinking. Then on December 20, 1973, almost two years exactly after his father died, Robert Tyre Jones III died of a heart attack. On May 23, 1975, Jones's widow was rushed to the Emory University Hospital with a bleeding peptic ulcer. She died in shock upon arrival in a hospital room. On October 13, 1977, Jones's youngest daughter, Mary Ellen Hood, died of cancer of the tongue and pharynx.

His eldest daughter, Clara Black, now lives quietly in Atlanta with her daughter, one of her three children. "I feel," she says, "I'm living on borrowed time."

PART SIX

Reunion and Farewell

18

It remains a lasting credit to the American and British people that when Bobby Jones came on the sporting scene, having conquered his thunderous temper, they instantly recognized the model athlete brought to life.

After his death, it also remains a lasting credit to his American and British friends and admirers that they proceeded to honor him in ways Jones himself would have called "courageous timidity"—ways he would most approve, that were in concert with his modest nature. Thus, the memorials to Bobby Jones are of a quiet kind, in keeping with the true spirit of the man—his integrity, his intellectual curiosity—as well as his deeds as an athlete.

At Emory University Law School there is the annual Robert Tyre Jones, Jr., Memorial Lecture on Legal Ethics. The inaugural lecture was given on October 31, 1974, by Mr. Justice Harry A. Blackmun of the United States Supreme Court. The following year the lecturer was Leon Jaworski. After that: Harvard University's professor of law and one of the leading authorities on the United States Consitution, Paul A. Freund; Alistair Cooke; and John A. Sibley, a leading Atlanta business and community leader.

In 1973 John H. MacDonnel, a Scot, suggested to his alma mater, the University of St. Andrews, that it would be a fitting memorial if the university built a Robert T. Jones, Jr., Hall. After much debate, the officers of St. Andrews believed it would be more financially suitable to set up a scholarship exchange program between St. Andrews and Emory. In 1976 they formed the Robert T. Jones, Jr., Memorial Trust, with Emory setting up its own trust to supplement the Scottish Trust. Then, in 1977, a tax-deductible fund, a counterpart of the Scottish Trust, was established in the United States, called the Robert T. Jones, Jr., Memorial Scholarship Fund. It was formed by Joseph C. Dey and W. Ward Foshay, two veteran powers of the USGA. Currently, there is a yearly exchange of eight students who are selected on the basis of scholastic ability, high standards of character, and leadership ability. A Jones scholar need not be a golfer or have any connection with the game.

Geographically, economically, and sociologically, the city of St. Andrews and the city of Atlanta have nothing in common; yet the citizens of both are bound by their deep respect and affection for Bobby Jones, a man who fifty years ago won the Grand Slam.

In October 1958, Bobby Jones was made a Freeman of the Royal Burgh of St. Andrews, the first American so honored since Dr. Benjamin Franklin in 1757. What it meant in so many homey ways was that Jones was free to feel as much at home in St. Andrews as in Atlanta.

Jones was going to St. Andrews as the nonplaying captain of the American team for the inaugural World Team Championship, a biannual event in which four of the best amateurs from each participating country (there were twenty-nine countries competing in 1958) play in a seventy-two-hole stroke-play event. Australia beat the United States in a play-off by two shots.

On September 9, in Atlanta, Jones received a cable from the Town Clerk of St. Andrews asking if he would be a Freeman of St. Andrews. Jones hadn't the foggiest notion what it was all about. He thought it was, perhaps, something like a key to the city, a nice political gesture. Whatever, Jones wanted very much to accept it.

When he and Mary, his son, and Mary Ellen, arrived in St. Andrews on October 3, Jones had a message waiting for him: the following day, the Town Clerk and the Provost wanted to meet with him to discuss the presentation plans. They met the next afternoon for an hour and a half. The more they talked of the honor, the more Jones knew it wasn't something to be taken lightly. This was further emphasized by the fact that, although the award ceremonies were six days away, on the evening of October 9, the Town Clerk wanted Jones's speech in writing as soon as possible. Suddenly, the matter was taking on alarming proportions.

Jones gave speeches the same way he played golf, by feel. All his acceptance speeches after a tournament were made up in his mind as the presenter of the trophy was giving his speech. At St. Andrews, Jones tried to write several speeches, but just couldn't get anything on paper. The Town Clerk became more and more nervous.

On Thursday afternoon, at Younger Graduation Hall, a

huge hall with a seating capacity of nearly 2,000, the Town Clerk again asked for Jones's speech. Jones apologized and stated it had been his experience that nothing could actually be written without the help of having the feel of the situation. The Town Clerk was worried, and again Jones had that terrible sense of fear, felt so often on the golf course, that he might look foolish, might draw a complete blank. He stuffed a few notes in his pocket for good measure.

All 116 players had received tickets to the ceremony; the rest had been sold to the townspeople in less than two hours. Jones could have filled an auditorium of 3,000.

With much pomp, the ceremony began at 8:00 P.M. A brief prayer was read, and then the Town Clerk, wearing the white wig of his office, read the citation. Following, the Provost, dressed in a crimson robe and wide ermine collar adorned with the magnificent chain of his office, spoke of Jones, his "enduring affection" for St. Andrews, and the golf Jones played there. He then presented Jones with a scroll, read by the Town Clerk, in a small silver casket adorned with the seal of the city of St. Andrews.

Jones, as if in the prime of youth, sprang up and walked the eight feet to the lectern. He realized he had no need for the notes in his pocket, that he would have no difficulty finding things to talk about to the people of St. Andrews. For it was to them he was going to talk; the players were only witnesses. This was Jones's reunion with the citizens of St. Andrews.

Jones spoke for almost fifteen minutes, going over his playing days at St. Andrews and telling his friends, "I could take out of my life everything except my experiences at St. Andrews and I'd still have a rich full life."

Then near the end of his speech it occurred to him to speak

about the words of friends and friendship, which he felt so sincerely were among the most important in the English language, and yet so loosely used. "Friends," he said, "are a man's priceless treasures, and life rich in friendship is full indeed."

"When I say," he said slowly, looking out among the audience, "with due regard for the meaning of the word, that I am your friend, I have pledged to you the ultimate in loyalty and devotion. In some respects friendship may even transcend love, for in true friendship there is no place for jealousy. When without more, I say that you are my friends, it is possible that I may be imposing upon you a greater burden than you are willing to assume. But when you have made me aware on many occasions that you have a kindly feeling toward me, and when you have honored me by every means at your command, then when I call you my friend, I am at once affirming my high regard and affection for you and declaring my complete faith in you and trust in the sincerity of your expressions. And so my fellow citizens of St. Andrews, it is with this appreciation of the full sense of the word that I salute you as my friends." Then everyone stood and sang "God Save the Queen."

Jones left the stage, got into an electric golf car, and was directed down the center aisle of Younger Graduation Hall. So emotionally stirred were the Scots by Jones's speech that for a moment a heavy silence filled the huge hall. Many in the audience had watched Jones win the 1927 British Open at St. Andrews, and had borne him on their shoulders triumphantly to the Royal and Ancient Clubhouse. They had cheered him all the way back to the clubhouse after he had won the British Amateur in 1930. On that warm July day in 1936, they had closed their shops and hung out signs "Our Bobby Is Back,"

247

and rushed onto the links to watch him play a casual round of golf. Once more, there was no holding back their deep affection and respect for Bobby Jones, and suddenly every Scot broke into an old Scottish song, "Will Ye No' Come Back Again."

Index

Index

Index